A History of Witchcraft

JEFFREY B. RUSSELL

A History of
Witchcraft

Sorcerers, Heretics, and Pagans

with 94 illustrations

THAMES AND HUDSON

For Carl T. Berkhout

Other books by Jeffrey B. Russell:

Dissent and Reform in the Early Middle Ages (1965)
Medieval Civilization (1968)
A History of Medieval Christianity: Prophecy and Order (1968)
Religious Dissent in the Middle Ages (1971)
Witchcraft in the Middle Ages (1972)
The Devil: Perceptions of Evil from Antiquity to Primitive
  Christianity (1977)

Frontispiece: Brujos, by Goya, *c.* 1794–5, showing witches' alleged powers of levitation. The conical hats, also used to designate heretics in the Middle Ages, may have their origins in the symbolism of the "horn of power" or fertility.

© 1980 Thames and Hudson Ltd, London
First published in the United States of America in 1980
by Thames and Hudson Inc.,
500 Fifth Avenue, New York, New York 10110

First paperback edition 1982
Reprinted 1987

Library of Congress Catalog card number 79-67541

Printed and bound in the German Democratic Republic

Contents

Preface   7

Introduction: What is a witch?   8

PART I   SORCERY AND HISTORICAL WITCHCRAFT   17

1 Sorcery   18

SORCERY WORLDWIDE   20
SORCERY IN ANCIENT TIMES   29
SORCERY AND RELIGION   33

2 The roots of European witchcraft   37

INTERPRETATIONS OF EUROPEAN WITCHCRAFT   40
SORCERY, FOLKLORE, AND RELIGION IN PAGAN EUROPE   42
THE LEGAL STATUS OF SORCERY   52

3 Witchcraft, heresy, and inquisition   55

THE DUALIST HERESIES   58
FROM SORCERY TO WITCHCRAFT   63

4 The witch-craze on the continent of Europe   72

THE GROWTH OF THE WITCH-CRAZE   76
THE CLIMAX OF THE WITCH-CRAZE   83

5 Witchcraft in Britain and America   90

WITCHCRAFT IN THE BRITISH ISLES   90
WITCHCRAFT IN THE AMERICAN COLONIES   103

6 Witchcraft and society   109

   WITCHCRAFT AND WOMEN   113
   THE SALEM TRIALS   118

7 The decline of witchcraft   122

   THE ROMANTIC REVIVAL   131

PART II   MODERN WITCHCRAFT   139

8 Survivals and revivals   140

   MODERN SORCERY   140
   SATANISM   144

9 The religion of the witches   148

   THE RISE OF NEOPAGAN WITCHCRAFT   148
   WITCHCRAFT AND THE FEMINIST MOVEMENT   155
   WITCHCRAFT TODAY   157

10 The role of witchcraft   172

Appendix   177

Notes   178

Bibliography   180

List of illustrations   184

Index   188

Preface

In Galicia, Spain, a popular phrase is *Yo no creo en brujas – pero hay*: 'I don't believe in witches – but they exist!' Whether or not one believes in the powers of witchcraft, one must believe in the existence of witches: I know quite a few of them personally. My own interest in witchcraft began in childhood and grew with my work in the history of religion. The present book deals with both historical and contemporary witchcraft. Portions of Chapter 3 appeared in different form in my earlier book, *Witchcraft in the Middle Ages* (Ithaca and London 1972), and in my article, 'Witchcraft and the demonization of heresy', *Mediaevalia*, 2 (1976), 1–21.

I would like to thank the many people who have helped me: Margot Adler, Rita Alcorn, Karen Alexander, Deborah Bender, Isaac Bonewits, Candice Haddad Campbell, Ann Forfreedom, Selena Fox, Magdalene Graham, Aidan Kelly, Johann Kruse, Gerard McCauley, Chris Ogden, George Patterson, Lynne Quiggin, Houston Roberts, C. R. Runyon, Hans Sebald, Marsha Smith, Mark Wyndham, Tim and Morning Glory Zell, Gwydion Penderwen, Jo and James, Rhea, Wolfe, and others who prefer not to be named.

My deepest debt is to Diana M. Russell, who worked with me at every stage of this book and who can claim much of whatever credit it may deserve.

Introduction: What is a witch?

Piffe martin

Marginal illustration to Martin Lefranc's *Champion des Dames*, about 1451. This is one of the earliest pictures of witches in medieval Europe. They are shown riding a broom and a stick through the air.

Opposite: the Wicked Witch of the West from *The Wizard of Oz* (1939). Dressed in black, wearing a conical hat, and threatening a child, the ugly crone is the stereotyped witch.

On 25 May 1978 Jack Anderson reported in a syndicated column headed 'Witches Invade the Military' that the United States Army had taken steps to ensure that their chaplains would be willing and able to minister to the increasing number of military personnel who were witches.

If you ask your acquaintances what a witch is, they are likely to tell you that witches do not exist. Witches, they will say, are imaginary old hags with warts on their noses, conical hats, broomsticks, and evil, cackling laughs. Walt Disney's wicked queen in *Snow White*, Margaret Hamilton's performance as the wicked witch in *The Wizard of Oz*, and behind them a long tradition of art stretching back through Goya to the thirteenth century, have fixed this image in our minds. Probably no living person ever fitted this stereotype.

Yet witches do exist.

Other acquaintances may say that a witch is a person having psychic powers. It is true that most witches claim psychic powers, but possession of such powers does not make one a witch. There is much more to witchcraft than that. Others may think that witches practise Voodoo, which is a misunderstanding of both witchcraft and Voodoo. Voodoo is a religion combining Christianity and African paganism: its rites are designed to protect *against* witchcraft and other evils.

More accurate and helpful answers are: (1) a witch is a sorcerer: this is the anthropological approach; (2) a witch is a Satanist: this is the historical approach; (3) a witch worships the ancient gods and practises magic: this is the approach favoured by modern witches. Each approach can be justified.

Someone hoping to delve deeper into the question will be helped little by most of the popular books that clog the occult sections of bookshops. One recent book deals with extrasensory perception, astrology, the Process Church, Satanism, Pentecostals, the Manson family, palmistry, *Hair*, spiritualism, UFOs, the tarot, and psychedelic drugs – as well as witches. Such a potpourri may be entertaining, but it is not very illuminating. Witchcraft is not the same as the occult, and many witches take pains to dissociate themselves from the occult.

The commonest misconception about witchcraft is that 'there is no such thing as a witch'. A whole traffic jam of other errors must also be cleared off the road before proceeding. 'A witch-doctor is a witch.' A witch-doctor or medicine man practises magic, but his function is to combat the threats or effects of witchcraft. 'Witchcraft is the same the world over.' In fact a great difference exists between the witchcraft of Europe and the sorcery of other cultures. 'Possession is related to witchcraft.' Possession is an internal attack

upon an individual by evil spirits, an invasion of the psyche; obsession is an external, physical attack. In neither does the victim make a conscious pact with the evil spirit. In diabolical witchcraft, on the other hand, the witch voluntarily invited the evil spirit through invocation or other means. Most modern witches eschew such invocation entirely. 'The black mass is an integral part of witchcraft.' The black mass is unknown in historical European witchcraft and rejected not only by contemporary witches but even by Satanists. The only time that the black mass was seriously performed was during the reign of Louis XIV, and even then it had no connection with contemporary witchcraft. 'Witchcraft is characteristic of the Middle Ages.' European witchcraft emerged only towards the end of the Middle Ages. The great witch-craze occurred during the Renaissance, Reformation, and seventeenth century. 'Witches are women, usually ugly old women.' Both in the past and in the present many men have practised witchcraft, and many female witches are quite young. 'Witchcraft is a silly and trivial subject.' During the witch-craze at least 100,000 people were tortured and killed as witches. Witch beliefs have had great psychological and sociological

A modern witch, Sybil Leek, with a witch doll from her antique shop.

Opposite: Goya, *Conjuro, c.* 1794–5. Goya, himself a sceptic, painted grotesque scenes of witchcraft for satirical purposes. Here the stereotyped witches are accompanied by familiars, stick pins in images, and carry a basket of dead babies for use in their cannibalistic orgy.

effects. Anthropologists, psychologists, and historians now treat witchcraft as a serious subject.

But what really is a witch? One answer lies in the roots and development of words. 'Witch' derives from the Old English *wicca* (pronounced 'witcha' and meaning 'male witch') and *wicce* ('female witch', pronounced 'witcheh') and from the verb *wiccian*, meaning 'to cast a spell'. Contrary to common belief among modern witches, it is not Celtic in derivation, and it has nothing to do with the Old English *witan*, 'to know', or any other word relating to 'wisdom' (see Appendix). The explanation that witchcraft means 'craft of the wise' is false.

The term 'warlock' derives from Old English *waer*, 'truth', and *leogan*, 'to lie'. Originally it meant any oath-breaker or traitor. About 1460 the term was equated with 'witch'. It always applied to female as well as male witches, and there is no justification for using 'warlock' as the male equivalent of female 'witch'. 'Witch' is applied to both sexes. 'Wizard', unlike 'witch', really does derive from Middle English *wis*, 'wise'. The word first appears about 1440, meaning a 'wise man or woman'; in the sixteenth and seventeenth centuries it designated a high magician, and only after 1825 was it used as the equivalent of 'witch'.

'Sorcerer' derives from the French *sorcier*, from Late Latin *sortiarius*, 'diviner'. In French, *sorcier* means both 'sorcerer' and 'witch'. The English word 'sorcery' was introduced in the fourteenth century and became common in the sixteenth. As in French, the English term has always been unclear: sometimes it refers to simple sorcery, sometimes to diabolical witchcraft. 'Magician' derives from French *magique*, Latin *magia*, and Greek *mageia*. The Greek word *magos* originally designated the Iranian astrologer-priests who accompanied the army of Xerxes into Greece. Used in English by the end of the fourteenth century, 'magic' has often implied a sophisticated intellectual system as opposed to the cruder practices of 'sorcery'.

The concepts behind the words also need to be clear. One concept is superstition. Witchcraft is not necessarily a superstition. Often a superstition is thought to be a belief not founded in whatever world view is current. This usage is unfortunate, because it helps rigidify and confine thought. The creed of one age is the superstition of another; many of our own current beliefs will one day be considered superstitions. It is much more helpful to define superstition as a belief not founded in *any coherent* world view. Medieval Catholics, ancient Iranians, and contemporary Dayaks are not necessarily more superstitious than modern Englishmen or Americans. If you hold a belief that you have thought through and placed in a coherent world view of your own, then that belief is not a superstition for you. If on the other hand you hold a belief loosely or uncritically and fail to set it properly in a coherent world picture, that belief is a superstition for you. The number of scientific, religious, and political superstitions today are no fewer than in the past. Some people are superstitious all of the time, and all people are superstitious some of the time. When witchcraft fits into a coherent view of the world, it is not a superstition.

The supernatural is another concept that needs consideration. Witchcraft is often thought to involve supernatural powers. But the boundary between the natural and the supernatural is continually being adjusted. In this process science has often created difficulties by declaring certain subjects unfit for scientific investigation, thus leaving them by default in the hands of the occultists. A few decades ago, extrasensory perception (ESP) was regarded as supernatural nonsense. Now, although some scepticism properly remains, many scientists admit that the alleged phenomena warrant careful investigation. In fact, everything that exists must be natural, whether science is able to demonstrate its existence or not. If, for example, angels exist, they are part of the natural order of the universe. The term 'supernatural' has no useful meaning.

'Unscientific' is a more helpful term, though even here the lines are blurred. Magic need not be thought of as an inferior brand of science. The Comtian theory that humanity progresses naturally from magic to religion to science, though widely accepted in the nineteenth century, is no longer adequate. Lynn Thorndike's monumental eight-volume *History of Magic and Experimental Science* was not idly named: he was fully aware that the origins of science lie in magic and that most of the great scientists of the medieval and early modern world were also magicians, a point reinforced by Frances Yates' *Giordano Bruno and the Hermetic Tradition.* The basis of magic is the belief in *kosmos,* an ordered and coherent universe in which all the parts are interrelated. This is also the basis of the principle of uniformity upon which so much scientific theory has been constructed. In a universe in which all parts are related and affect one another, however remotely, there is a relationship between the individual human being and the stars, plants, minerals, and other natural phenomena. This is the magical belief in correspondence. Such doctrines have been carefully worked out in a coherent and sophisticated pattern. This sophisticated magic is called high magic.

Yet a fundamental difference between high magic and science does exist. Magic is not usually submitted to the tests of empirical investigation or Humian scepticism. It therefore has a validation problem. There are paths to truth other than the scientific and empirical. But on every path the rules of critical thought must be used to test every assertion. The most important principle is simple: the more an alleged phenomenon differs from ordinary experience, the greater the evidence is needed to overcome scepticism. If my secretary tells me that my daughter called me on the phone, I have few doubts that the message is accurate. If she says that the prime minister of Canada has called, my doubts are considerable, and if she tells me that the Virgin Mary is on the line, I am very hard to convince. Many books by magicians and occultists are inattentive to these simple rules of evidence. That is the validation problem. If someone tells you she has made an astral voyage to Alpha Centauri, or that he has seen an intergalactic spacecraft, your belief should be suspended until the evidence presented is overwhelming. Magic, like science, seeks knowledge, but its methods of attaining knowledge usually appear incoherent.

The high, intellectual magic of the astrologers and diviners is not an integral part of the history of witchcraft. During the great witch-craze in Europe few people were accused both of high magic and of witchcraft. The two traditions are distinct. Nonetheless, witchcraft does depend in part upon the magical world view that there are hidden relationships between all elements of the cosmos. The power that the witch or sorcerer exerts is presumed to be a natural power gained through the witch's or sorcerer's understanding of, and ability to control, these hidden relationships.

Quite different from the sophisticated systems of high magic is magic employed almost technologically to attain practical ends. This is low magic, or simple sorcery. Simple sorcery is automatic magic: one performs a certain action, and one gets results accordingly. One man practises sorcery, another technology: one man fertilizes a field by slitting a hen's throat over it at midnight, another by spreading steer manure over it at dawn.

Some anthropologists make no distinction between witchcraft and sorcery. Others, following Evans-Pritchard, use an African distinction between maleficent magicians who use material objects such as herbs or blood in their evil spells and those who injure others by means of an inherent and invisible quality they possess. These anthropologists assign the English word 'sorcerer' to the former and 'witch' to the latter. The distinction is valid, but the choice of English words arbitrary. Most historians distinguish between European witchcraft, which was a form of diabolism, and worldwide sorcery, which involves not veneration but exploitation of evil spirits. The English word *wicca*, 'witch', which appears in a manuscript first in the ninth century, originally meant 'sorcerer', but during the witch-craze it was used as the equivalent of the Latin *maleficus*, diabolical witch. Modern witches take a tack quite different from either anthropologists or historians. For them, witchcraft is the survival or the revival of ancient paganism. Modern witches differ from historical witches because they reject belief both in the Christian God and the Christian Devil. They differ from sorcerers in their emphasis upon worship of the gods rather than upon magic.

None of these usages can be declared absolutely correct. This book uses the term 'sorcery' for the sorcery practised round the world whether beneficent or maleficent, and whether mechanical or invoking spirits. It uses 'witchcraft' to mean either the diabolical witchcraft of the witch-craze or modern, neopagan witchcraft.

Sorcery is widespread in many societies. It must therefore perform useful functions, or else it would wither away. One function of sorcery is to relieve social tensions. Simple sorcery, at least when beneficent, is frequently part of the generally accepted religious fabric of society. Belief in sorcery helps define and sustain social values. It provides explanations of frightening events and terrifying phenomena. It gives the individual a sense of power over a mystifying and frightening world. Even belief in malevolent sorcery has a function. It helps affirm the boundaries of the community and enhances its solidarity against evil outsiders. When the sorcerer is identified as a hostile outsider, driving her out of the community or otherwise persecuting her gives the orthodox a sense of comradeship and self-justification. Once she is identified as a scapegoat, society can project upon her every kind of repressed evil. And guilt compounds the hostility: since she has been excluded, she must be guilty; she must be horrible and incarnate all that we hate. Sorcery may also serve as a strange system of justice, a way of righting wrongs, of getting even: curses are usually employed by the weak against the strong, whom they cannot otherwise hurt. And at the most personal level, sorcery may have the function of making the alleged victim the centre of attention and sympathy.

In periods of dislocation and dissolution of values, sorcery and witchcraft may have the additional function of providing a focus and a name for diffuse anxieties. In such conditions scapegoating becomes intense, as it did during the European witch-craze, when the insecurities and terrors of society were projected upon certain individuals who could then be tortured, killed, and so removed.

Another approach is 'to relate different ideas and behaviour concerning witchcraft to the structure of the societies where they have been studied.'[1] Mary Douglas and others have identified in the sorcery of diverse societies characteristic patterns of accusation deriving from the tensions in particular social relationships. Rather than relieving social tensions, sorcery beliefs may prolong and exacerbate them. Such beliefs arise from family divisions and feuds or from contests for authority within families or groups. A cliché of anthropology is that 'witchcraft accusations are not random', but rather follow observable social lines.[2]

Many modern historians have adapted anthropological methodology to the study of sorcery and witchcraft. Keith Thomas and Alan Macfarlane have done this for English witchcraft, Erik Midelfort and E. William Monter for continental witchcraft, and Paul Boyer and Stephen Nissenbaum for America. As Boyer and Nissenbaum comment, 'Historians . . . have begun more fully to realize how much information the study of "ordinary" people living in "ordinary" communities can bring to the most fundamental historical questions.' Boyer and Nissenbaum used 'the interaction of [this] "ordinary" history and the extraordinary moment [the Salem trials of 1692] to understand the epoch which produced them both.'[3] This new approach has added greatly to the understanding of historical witchcraft. Other historians, such as Norman Cohn, Richard Kieckhefer, and I, have followed a path closer to the history of ideas. Whatever the approach, the resurgence during the past two decades of interest in the history of European witchcraft has been extraordinary. Each approach has its value. To attempt to follow them all would be to blur the issues. I use the history of concepts, which defines witchcraft as the tradition of what it has been thought to be. The idea of witchcraft develops through time, and the development is discernible as a historical pattern.[4]

This development begins in worldwide sorcery.

A wooden Congolese image stuck with pins. The dividing line between magic and religion is sometimes weak. Pins may be thrust into an image to cause pain or, as here, to release the power of the deity.

1 Sorcery

Sorcery occurs in almost every society in the world. It is also the oldest and deepest element in the historical concept of European witchcraft, which was formed out of pagan religion, folklore, Christian heresy, and theology.

As with all magic, sorcery is based on the assumption that the cosmos is a whole and that hidden connections therefore exist among all natural phenomena. The sorcerer attempts through his knowledge and power to control or at least influence these connections in order to effect the practical results he desires. Closely related to sorcery is divination, the determination of facts or prediction of future events on the basis of the secret links between human beings on the one hand and herbs, stones, stars, the liver of a sheep, or the tracks of a jackal on the other. Though divination is close to sorcery, I distinguish between them for the purpose of tracing the origins of European witchcraft. In Europe, diviners entered a tradition that brought them close to high magic, while witchcraft took a different path.

The simplest sorcery is the mechanical performance of one physical action in order to produce another: tying a knot in a cord and placing it under a bed to cause impotence; performing sexual intercourse in a sown field in order to increase the harvest; thrusting pins into an image in order to cause pain or injury. The meaning of a given action varies among societies: thrusting pins into an image of a deity, for example, may be designed to release the deity's power rather than to cause anyone harm.

More complex sorcery goes beyond mechanical means and invokes the aid of spirits. If a member of the Lugbara tribe in Uganda is injured, he goes to the shrines of his dead ancestors and invokes their aid; the ghosts will issue forth and punish the culprit. The distinction between this invocational sorcery and religion is sometimes fuzzy, but in the main the sorcerer tries to compel, rather than to implore, the powers that be to do his bidding.

The thought processes of sorcery are intuitive rather than analytical. They may derive, for example, from the individual's observations of single critical incidents. A critical incident is an emotionally charged experience. In a state of rage, you wish your father dead and strike a pillow in imitation of a blow aimed against him. The next day you learn that he has suddenly died. Even in a materialistic society, you will probably feel guilt, and when you assume a universe of hidden connections, the guilt is likely to be intense, for you may believe that your action really did cause the death. Critical events that an empirical methodology ignores because they cannot be replicated and empirically verified may be assumed to be significant in a magical world view. Sorcery beliefs may also arise from unconscious thought expressed in dreams and visions. In dreams one being or person shifts and merges into

another, and many other strange events occur. In societies where dreams are taken seriously and distinctions between dream and physical reality are blurred, dreams and visions have great power to persuade. In most societies, detailed sets of beliefs regarding sorcery are handed down by tradition and become part of the social and psychological systems of individuals. Those individuals will then all the more readily accept critical incidents and dreams as confirmation of the traditions. Linkages hidden to the empirical or analytical observer may appear obvious to the intuitive thinker.

Often sorcery has an integral function in society. In some societies it is closely related to religion. A priest or priestess of a public religion may perform ritual acts to make rain, ripen the harvest, procure peace, or secure success in the hunt or victory in war. So long as these acts are public and social in intent, sorcery may be a handmaid of religion. But when the sorcerer's acts are performed privately for the benefit of individuals rather than

Evidence for the practice of simple sorcery in Europe. A brown Bellarmine jug containing a cloth heart stuck with pins, human hair, and nail parings. Found at Westminster ten feet below street-level during excavations in 1904.

Sia curing ceremony. A sick boy of the Pueblo Indian Sia tribe undergoes magical treatment in 1889 in the ceremonial chamber of the Giant society. In some societies illness is often regarded as resulting from sorcery.

of society they are antisocial and do not form part of religion. In some cults, Voodoo for example, or Macumba in Brazil, the distinctions are not clear, but usually societies distinguish legally between public, religious sorcery and private sorcery, approving the one and outlawing the other.

The effects of sorcery can be real for those who believe in it. Volunteers from technologically advanced countries seeking to serve in societies where sorcery is taken seriously are often asked the question: a man in your village is suddenly seized by severe cramps; whom do you call, the physician or the witch-doctor? The proper answer is that you call both. The cause of the pain may be purely physical, but if the man believes himself to be bewitched, his fear may produce or sharpen the pain.

SORCERY WORLDWIDE

Such are the general characteristics of sorcery. Its particulars vary from society to society. One of the first thorough anthropological investigations of sorcery was made by E. E. Evans-Pritchard, who studied the Zande of the southern

A witch-doctor of the Zande in the late 1920s. Photograph by the anthropologist E. Evans-Pritchard.

Sudan. The Zande distinguished three varieties of magic. The first was good, benevolent magic, which included the consultation of oracles and diviners, the use of amulets for protection against charms, rites to procure the fertility of crops, and even *bagbuduma*, homicidal magic, so long as it was limited to revenge upon those who had slain one's kin. Good magic was used to procure justice as understood by Zande society, and *bagbuduma* was rendered ineffective when employed to unjust purpose. Sorcery, on the other hand, was unjust. Sorcery was the use of magic, especially magic using material objects, in order to harm those whom one hated for no just reason. Sorcery was a form of unjust aggression springing from jealousy, envy, greed, or other base human desires. Sorcery worked magic in an antisocial fashion and was condemned by Zande society. Evans-Pritchard called the third variety of magic 'witchcraft'. This 'witchcraft' was an internal power inherited by a man from his father or by a woman from her mother. The source of this power, or *mangu*, existed physically inside the 'witch's' stomach or attached to his liver, as an oval, blackish swelling in which various small objects might be found, or as a round, hairy ball with teeth.

Zande witches had meetings at which they feasted and practised evil magic together. They made a special ointment which they rubbed on their skins in order to render themselves invisible. They rode out at night either in spirit or in their bodies. Often the witch was supposed to lie in bed at night with his spouse while sending out his spirit to join the other witches in eating the souls of the victims. Sometimes the witches attacked the victim physically, tearing off pieces of his flesh to devour in their secret meetings. Anyone having a slow, wasting disease was likely to be the victim of the witch. Witch cats had sexual relations with women. The powers of the Zande witches were enormous:

If blight seizes the groundnut crop it is witchcraft; if the bush is vainly scoured for game it is witchcraft; if a wife is sulky and unresponsive to her husband it is witchcraft; if a prince is cold and distant with his subject it is witchcraft; if, in fact, any failure or misfortune falls upon anyone at any time and in relation to any of the manifold activities of his life it may be due to witchcraft.[5]

The Zande employed diviners and medicine men to protect them from witches and cure them of the effects of witchcraft.

The Bechuana of Botswana distinguish between day-sorcerers, who practise sorcery only irregularly on specific occasions and usually for pay, and the more terrifying night-witches, who are accompanied by familiars in the form of animals (usually owls). The night-witches are universally malicious and cast their spells over one and all. They are generally thought of as elderly women. The Basuto, a Bantu tribe in South Africa, also distinguish between two groups of sorcerers, one of which consists mainly of women who fly out at night, ride 'on sticks or on fleas, meet in assemblies, and dance stark naked'.[6] In other societies, sorcerers are variously accused of cannibalism, incest, nymphomania, and other activities offensive to society.

The variation in sorcery among different societies is natural. What is surprising is the degree of similarity. The similarity between many African witch beliefs and those of historical Europe are pronounced. Both African and European 'witchcraft' include the following characteristics: the witch is generally female and often elderly. The witches meet in assemblies at night, leaving their bodies or changing their shapes in order to fly to the meeting-place. The witch sucks the blood of victims or devours their organs, causing them to waste away. Witches eat children or otherwise cause their deaths, sometimes bringing their flesh to the assembly. They ride out on brooms or other objects, fly naked through the air, use ointments to change their shapes, perform circular dances, possess familiar spirits, and practise orgy. Of course no one group of sorcerers is supposed to do all these things, but all these beliefs may be found in Europe as well as in Africa. In all, at least fifty different motifs of European witchcraft can be found in other societies.[7]

The worldwide similarity of sorcery beliefs constitutes the most curious and important dilemma in the study of witchcraft. When we find, centuries and continents apart, the idea of a night-hag seducing men and murdering children or a sorceress riding a broomstick, we are not entitled to dismiss the question of how these similarities arise.

Opposite: a witch-mask from the Sankuru River area representing a spiritual power who is invoked in the periodic witch-hunting drives of the Songe, southern Zaire.

Possible explanations of the similarities include (1) coincidence; (2) cultural diffusion; (3) archetypal/structural inheritance; (4) the existence of an ancient and coherent world religion of witchcraft. The volume of the evidence over such a wide variety of cultures and geographies through millennia renders coincidence virtually impossible. On the other hand, postulating a world religion of witchcraft ignores the enormous dissimilarities that also exist among societies and the fact that no evidence of any explicit connections exists. The explanation of archetypal or structural inheritance is an open option. It is certain that the structure of the human brain is determined by genetic patterns and probable that the structures of the mind are therefore also genetically inherent. Worldwide similarities of mental structure derived from the common human gene pool may then exist. It is possible (though far from demonstrated) that such similar mental structures produce archetypes, or similar responses to similar ideas. Jungians argue, for example, that everyone responds to the notion of 'the wise old man', the kindly and benevolent older person there to guide us. The image of such a wise old man varies from culture to culture (Tolkien's Gandalf presumably would strike no deep chords in Botswana), but the underlying archetype is universal. Yet the worldwide similarities in sorcery beliefs exceed those that these theories would predict. Cultural diffusion, the exchange of ideas among societies, is doubtless part of the answer. But the number and detail of the similarities across wide gulfs of time and geography is astounding. The puzzle remains.

The problem has several direct implications for the interpretation of European witchcraft. Many recent historians have explained witchcraft solely as a variety of Christian heresy or as an invention of scholastics and inquisitors, dismissing as unimportant its similarities to the sorcery of other cultures. This has led to an overstatement of the Christian elements and an improper isolation of the phenomenon. The anthropologists on the other hand have tended to understate the Christian elements. The truth lies somewhere in between: sorcery, similar to that existing worldwide, is the oldest and most basic element in historical European witchcraft, but other elements gradually transformed European sorcery into diabolical witchcraft.

Anthropologists and historians have done much to illuminate the social history of sorcery. In Africa, sorcery is more commonly practised by women than by men, but witch-doctors or curers are more frequently men. Accusations of sorcery generally appear in situations of tension within families or groups, particularly in turbulent and unsettled periods. Accusations pass frequently among wives in polygamous households, and between mothers-in-law and daughters-in-law. Accusations are lodged against old and young alike, but older persons are more likely to be singled out, perhaps because age and infirmity have rendered them unsociable, perhaps simply because they are weak. A common charge is that an old person has prolonged his life by devouring the bodies or souls of children. Anyone who is notably strange or unsociable is prone to accusation. Boyer and Nissenbaum's recent study of Salem witchcraft emphasized the importance of local geography and local religious politics in influencing the pattern of sorcery charges.

Cultural differences in determining patterns of witch accusations have been observed by anthropologists. Among the Nyakyusa of southern Tan-zania sorcerers may be of either sex. They are chiefly accused of eating the in-ternal organs of sleeping neighbours and of drying up the milk of cattle. On the other hand Pondo sorcerers, in the Cape province of South Africa, are women; their most common crime is having sexual intercourse with familiar spirits. The apparent reason for the difference is that the Nyakyusa are sexually secure but nutritionally insecure, so that they envy their neighbours' food and attribute their nourishment to illicit eating, while the Pondo, who are sexually more insecure, express their fears more in terms of sex than of food.

Just as the expression of witchcraft may change from society to society depending on its function, so its function may change over time in one society. The Bakweri of the western Cameroon, for example, were deeply afraid of sorcery in the period preceding the 1950s. Racked by ambivalence about riches and poverty, by a sense of collective guilt about the decline of their power and status, and by the fear that their low fertility rate would cause them to die out, they were dominated by jealousies that translated into fear of sorcery. In the 1950s their economic status improved remarkably owing to a boom in their major crop, bananas, and the period of prosperity brought first a purge of suspected sorcerers and then, the catharsis over, a decline in accusations and in belief in sorcery generally. During the 1960s, when the Bakweri suffered an economic setback, a resurgence of fear and accusations occurred.

Witch-doctors, medicine men, and *curanderos* ('witch-doctors' of Mexico and south-west USA), whose job it is to control and thwart sorcery, form part of the pattern of sorcery beliefs. The tribal chief, village headman, or other authorities are invested with the responsibility of protecting their people from the effects of sorcery. Witch detectors (called 'oracles' by anthropologists) are consulted in order to identify and foil evil sorcerers. 'The Nyoro, in the west of Uganda, consult men who they believe are possessed by spirits (called *mbandwa*) and reveal secret matters as their mouthpieces.'[8] A diviner may also be consulted: he does not speak with the voice of a spirit but 'interprets the answer that is supposed to be given by the behaviour of the mechanical objects he uses.'[9] A message may be read in the paths of the planets or in the tracks of beasts. Dances or other rituals, such as those of the *ndakó-gboyá* dancers of the Nupe, may serve to detect and drive off evil spirits and evil sorcerers. The *ndakó-gboyá* dancers wore tall, cylindrical disguises and identified sorcerers by nodding these weird shapes at them. In other cults, the witch-doctors identify the sorcerers from a line of villagers by looking at them in a mirror and then use their enormous social powers to extract confessions from those they have selected. Such witch-cleansing activities spread in times of stress when whole communities feel the need of protection against sorcery. Whole cults, such as that of the *ndakó-gboyá*, may arise in such a time. These cults, practising a relatively simple ritual intended to detect and neutralize the power of evil sorcerers, lack formal structure, organization, and doctrine, and easily cross ethnic boundaries and adapt themselves to the traditions of different peoples.

In Central Africa and in Central America anthropologists have found that communities which are small and in which the social structure is tightly knit are particularly prone to sorcery beliefs, because they feel surrounded and threatened. Their fears increase whenever internal relations are confused or when the society is under unusually strong external pressure. This is why in some societies sorcery accusations increased at least temporarily during the period of European colonialism. In larger communities, or where social associations are freer and escape from unwanted ties easier, as in nomadic societies, sorcery beliefs are less common. The beliefs vary in intensity, kind, and function as social patterns vary, but anthropologists have not been able to correlate specific kinds of belief with particular kinds of social patterns. Much work remains to be done in this field. With all its variations, sorcery is widely believed in and widely practised. It speaks to human needs for justice, protection, and revenge in a world that too often seems out of our control.

Some similarities between European witchcraft and non-European sorcery result from the exportation of European ideas through colonialism. Voodoo is an example. Voodoo began as a religion brought to Haiti by slaves imported from the Benin coast (the name is a corruption of the Yoruba word for 'god'). Under the influence of Christianity and other European ideas it became

a syncretistic religion that has blended together not only different African cults but also certain beliefs from European folklore. . . . In short, this is a sort of conglomeration of elements of all kinds, dominated by African traditions. This religion is practiced by ninety percent of the Haitian people. . . . At the same time these people consider themselves Catholic.[10]

The basis of the religion is the worship of *loa* (gods or spirits). The Catholic Church has diligently attacked Voodoo, equating the *loa* with demons, but the people have resisted such identifications. As a Haitian peasant told an inquiring anthropologist, 'To serve the *loa* you have to be a Catholic.'[11]

Voodooists distinguish between worship of the *loa*, which is a religion, and the practice of magic. All magic is considered black. It may be worked mechanically or with the help of the *loa*. The *loa* may thus be bent to evil ends, but it is to the *loa* that one must also turn for protection against evil magic. Prayers to the *loa* and magical invocations of the *loa* are difficult to distinguish. Voodoo sorcery, a mélange of European and African ideas, includes incantations, spells, the use of images, rain-making, and a cult of the dead. One of its more peculiar beliefs is the concept of zombies, 'the living dead', corpses who are exhumed and made by sorcerers to walk and do their bidding. Voodoo sorcery also contains a number of elements probably derived from Europe. Sorcerers may slay children at their ritual meetings or else catch them at night in their homes and suck their blood. Sorcerers rub their bodies with an ointment that removes their skin so that they may fly in the air. Shooting stars are really sorcerers in flight. Sorcerers change their shape into wolves, pigs, horses, or black cats.

This mixture of European and African elements is an advanced example of the syncretism found in other societies colonialized by Europeans. It is difficult to distinguish native from imported elements. For example, belief in

Opposite above: Voodoo dancers in Haiti build up to a trance. In Voodoo, elements of Christianity, paganism, and magic combine to create a unique religion.

Opposite below: Rapedi Letsebe, magician and rainmaker of the Kgatla tribe in Botswana, with his divining bones. A photograph taken in the 1920s.

Three witches, changing their shapes, fly off through the air to a sabbat. A late fifteenth-century woodcut. Belief in shape-shifting or lycanthropy was connected with witchcraft in Europe, and witches were believed to have the power, with the Devil's assistance, to change their shapes and take animal forms.

shape-shifting is common worldwide as well as in Europe, though the emphasis in Haiti on wolves and black cats suggests strong European influence. Anthropologists have described how actual experiences during cult practices may have reinforced belief in shape-shifting. 'At night huge fires were lit in [the] camp; naked women carried out hideous dances round the fires . . . twisting their bodies into frightening shapes.'[12] Another

European observer saw a Voodoo priest possessed by the spirit of the Haitian 'emperor' Desselines: 'It was the man himself. . . . I saw the ferocious face, the fanatic cast of countenance, and the whole body moulded in a vengeful attitude.'[13] Such powers of unconscious imitation account for the strength of the worldwide belief in shape-shifting.

SORCERY IN ANCIENT TIMES

Though European witchcraft influenced sorcery in modern non-European societies, non-European societies had little demonstrated influence on the development of European witchcraft. But the ancient Near East, Greece, and Rome also had similar beliefs, and from these civilizations came many of the ideas on which European witchcraft was based. Throughout there was a blurring of sorcery with demonology. Characteristics assigned to a demon might also be assigned to a witch. For example, the devouring hag Lilitu (see below) was a spirit, but her characteristics were transferred in the Middle Ages to the diabolical witch.

The Sumerians and Babylonians invented an elaborate demonology. They believed that the world was full of spirits and that most of them were hostile. Each person had a tutelary spirit to protect him from demonic enemies. Among the most terrible Sumerian demons was Ardat Lili or Lilitu, a cousin of the Graeco-Roman Lamia and the prototype of the Hebrew Lilith. Lilitu was a frigid, barren female spirit with wings and taloned hands and feet; accompanied by owls and lions she swept shrieking through the night, seducing sleeping men or drinking their blood. Another female demon, Labartu, went out with a serpent in each hand and attacked children and their mothers or nurses. Against such powers every kind of magic was needed, including amulets, incantations, and exorcisms, but especially the protection of the tutelary deity, for 'the man who hath not a god as he walketh in the street, the demon covers him as a garment'.[14]

The world view of ancient Egypt was less terrifying. Gods and spirits were all part of the one, living cosmos, and no distinction was made between natural and supernatural. The sorcerer used his wisdom and knowledge of amulets, spells, formulas, and figures to bend the cosmic powers to his purpose or that of his clients. As all spirits were part of the cosmic whole, none was evil, but the sorcerer could turn spiritual powers in ways that could harm his adversaries as well as benefiting himself.

The two most influential sources of European thought in general were the Classical Graeco-Roman and the Hebrew. The Greeks created both philosophy and a sophisticated system of magic. The highest form of magic in Greece was *theourgia*, literally 'working things pertaining to the gods'. A high, benevolent magic, theurgy was close to religion. A lower grade of magic, *mageia*, was much closer to sorcery. Originally a *magos* was an astrologer from Iran, or else a Greek following the high magical tradition of the Iranians. But by the end of the fifth century BC the *magoi* had already gained a reputation for harmful sorcery and even fraud: Plato viewed them as a menace to society. The *magoi* were private individuals claiming the technical knowledge and powers to help their clients and harm their clients'

enemies by performing certain rites or supplying certain formulas. Lower than the *magoi* were the *goëtes*, practitioners of a crude, lowbrow variety of magic. 'Howlers' of incantations, mixers of potions, and weavers of spells, the practitioners of *goëteia* had a wide reputation for charlatanism.

The Roman authorities were generally intolerant of all varieties of sorcery. The practice of sorcery, as opposed to the approved public rites connected with religion, was viewed as a threat to society. The emperors, always terrified of plots against their lives, feared sorcery as the least detectable and therefore most dangerous threat. Repression was indiscriminately harsh. A young man seen in the public baths touching first the marble tiles and then his chest while repeating the seven Greek vowels, a spell prescribed against stomach trouble, was arrested, tortured, and executed. The harsh tradition of Roman law was one of the foundations upon which the medieval prosecution of witchcraft was based.

The image of the sorcerer in Classical literature is almost uniformly dark: Circe the seductress, Medea the murderess, Ovid's Dipsias, Apuleius' Oenothea, and especially the Canidia and Sagana of Horace, who with pale and hideous faces, naked feet, dishevelled hair, and clothed in rotting shrouds, meet at night in a lonely place to claw the soil with their taloned fingers, rip apart a black lamb, eat its flesh, and invoke the gods of the underworld. This literary tradition of the evil sorceress readily supported the later Christian image of the witch.

Graeco-Roman thought also began the close linking of sorcery with demonology that became the dominant characteristic of European witchcraft. The Greeks believed that all varieties of sorcerer worked their trade by consulting *daimones*. The Greek *daimōn*, from which our word 'demon' is derived, was used by Homer almost as a synonym for *theos*, 'god'. After Homer, the word came to mean a spiritual being inferior to a god. At the time of Socrates, a *daimōn* could be either good or evil, and Socrates himself claimed to have a *daimōn* that whispered good advice into his ear. But when Plato's pupil Xenocrates divided the spiritual world into gods and demons, he shifted the dark qualities of the gods on to the demons, who henceforth were considered evil. The sorcerers' consultation of demons then linked them firmly with the powers of darkness.

Other elements of Graeco-Roman religion also contributed to the formation of the image of the witch. Lamias, spirits who like Lilitu roamed the world seducing men and killing infants, and Harpies, winged women who swept the world on the wind perpetrating gross indignities, bequeathed their characteristics to the human witch. The festivals of Dionysos became a blueprint for the rites allegedly practised by the medieval witches. The Dionysian rites took place at night, often in a cave or grotto, locations connected with fertility and the powers of the underworld. The worshippers were usually women led by a male priest. The procession bore torches and a phallic image, and led a dark goat or its image. The goat, symbol of fertility, represented Dionysos, who was usually portrayed as shaggy and horned. The rite concluded in wine-drinking, ecstatic dancing, and animal sacrifice.

Human sacrifice, made much of in literature, probably did not actually extend into historical times. Accusations of orgy against the Dionysiacs are

Opposite: a terracotta plaque depicting Lilitu, the malevolent female spirit of the Sumerians and prototype of the Hebrew Lilith. Lilitu flew out at night, sometimes accompanied by owls and lions (as here), had sexual relations with sleeping men, and slew children and babies. These characteristics were later transferred to the medieval witch. Early second millennium BC.

Festival of Dionysos: satyrs with Dionysos and a maenad. Amphora by the Amasis painter, sixth century BC. The orgiastic rites of Dionysos, which appeared in Rome as the Bacchanalia, were a prototype of the witches' sabbat.

also exaggerated, but in the Hellenistic period orgiastic practices seem to have spread, and the rites of Cybele and the Magna Mater were characterized by ecstatic dancing and sexual frenzy. The Roman version of the rites of Dionysos, the Bacchanalia, became so notorious for licence that it was outlawed by the Senate in 186 BC. The historian Livy's description of the Bacchanalia became an important part of the literary tradition of European witchcraft: men and women were said to meet at night and to celebrate by torchlight rites including orgiastic feasting, drinking, and sex. It is difficult to say how much of this is true. Similar accusations were lodged against any group perceived as a secret society. Not only religious groups, such as the Dionysiacs, but also clandestine political groups, such as Catiline and his conspirators, were frequently accused of orgy and cannibalism.

Hebrew sorcery, largely derived from that of the Canaanites and Babylonians, had a great though indirect influence on European witchcraft. When the Hebrew Bible was translated into Greek, Latin, and modern tongues, the meaning of the Hebrew words underwent transformation. Sometimes the translations promoted persecutions. The most important case in point is Exodus 22:18, which in the original Hebrew ordains that a *kashaph* be put to death. A *kashaph* was a magician, diviner, or sorcerer, but nothing resembling a diabolist. In the Latin Vulgate, the Hebrew was translated as *Maleficos non patieris vivere*, 'You shall not permit *maleficos* to live'. At the time the Vulgate translation was made, the term *maleficus* itself was still vague: it could mean any kind of criminal, though it was frequently applied to malevolent sorcerers. As the European witch-craze developed, *maleficus* came specifically to denote a diabolical witch, and the text was used as proof and justification for the execution of witches. And that was not the end of the transformation. The translators of the King James Bible (1611) rendered most references to Hebrew sorcerers by the English word 'wizard', connoting a magician or sorcerer. But James I, who authorized the new translation, had expressed violent hatred of witches in his book *Demonolatry*. For the king, a witch was a member of a diabolical cult and had made a pact with Satan. He wanted witches exterminated, and his translators deliberately translated *kashaph* as 'witch' in order to provide clear biblical sanctions for their execution. The 'witch' of Endor whom King Solomon consulted was originally a *ba'alath ob*, 'mistress of a talisman'; in the Latin she was a *mulierem habentem pythonem*, 'a woman possessing an oracular spirit'; but in the King James version she too appears as a sinister 'witch'. Thus Hebrew sorcery was transformed to fit the prejudices of Christian demonology.

SORCERY AND RELIGION

Hebrew sorcery was far from diabolism, but Hebrew religion was influential in creating the concept of the Devil. Most world religions were and are monist, postulating one divine principle which is both good and evil. The gods were manifestations of this one principle, so they too were morally ambivalent. Perhaps the best illustration of this ambivalence is the figure of the Mexican god Quetzalcoatl, who is life and death, love and destruction. The first major break with monism occurred about 600 BC with the teachings of Zarathushtra in Iran. Zarathushtra's revelation was that evil is not a manifestation of the divine at all; rather it proceeds from a wholly different source. This religious dualism posits the existence of two principles, one goodness and light, the other darkness and evil. Mazdaism, the religion derived from Zarathushtra's thought, had enormous influence on both Greek and Hebrew thought, and through them on Christianity.

Eastern religions such as Hinduism and Buddhism continue to profess one or another form of monism, but Western religions are monotheistic religions modified by dualism. A spectrum of Western religions goes from the extreme dualism of Mazdaism through Gnosticism, Manicheism, Christianity, Judaism, and Islam (where dualism is very attenuated). All these religions, however different from one another, posit a God who is wholly good and omnipotent yet who paradoxically tolerates evil, which is a force or at least a void in opposition to or limitation of the good God.

The problem of evil has always been the most difficult problem of Judaeo-Christian theology. How is it that God can be all-powerful and all-good yet create a world in which cancer, famine, and torture are abundant? One answer is that evil is at least in part caused by an evil spirit of great power. The Hebrews named this spirit the *satan*, 'the obstructor'. *Satan* was translated into Greek as *diabolos*, from which came the Latin *diabolus* and the English 'devil'.* The figure of Satan emerged only gradually and unclearly in the Old Testament, but later, in the period of Apocalyptic and Apocryphal literature (200 BC to AD 150), it received sharp definition. Judaism remained

*Contrary to a widespread belief among modern witches, the word 'devil' is not related to 'divinity' and does not mean 'little god'. The Indo-European roots of the two words are completely different: *gwel* for 'devil' and *deiw* for 'divine'.

The Mexican god Quetzalcoatl. This two-sided figure symbolizes the
ambivalence of the deity in monist religions: the god is both life-giving and death-
dealing. In Judaeo-Christianity, the evil aspects were separated from the god and
devolved upon the Devil.

monotheistic, so that Satan could never become a fully independent principle as his counterpart had in Mazdaism, but the power that Apocalyptic Judaism assigned to him was considerable. The Lord and the Devil were perceived as being in ethical and cosmic opposition. Each has his own kingdom: that of the Lord is light, while that of Satan is darkness. The Devil's plan is to lure Israel away from Yahweh, and he enjoys some successes, but at the end of the world Israel will repent, and the Messiah will bring the kingdom of the Devil to an end. Meanwhile the Devil heads a host of fallen angels and evil spirits who roam the world seeking the ruin and destruction of souls.

This concept of the world transforms the concept of sorcery. At its simplest, sorcery was purely mechanical. Then it was linked to the invocation of spirits. Then the spirits were defined as hostile to humanity. Now they were defined as hostile to God. Apocalyptic Judaism perceived the spirits as evil demons in league with one another under the generalship of the Devil, the principle of evil. It followed from this belief that a sorcerer who invokes spirits is calling upon the servants of Satan. Christianity made the argument air-tight. Good spirits such as angels and saints could not be compelled, Christians argued, but only supplicated. The only spirits that could be compelled were evil spirits. A sorcerer compelled spirits; therefore, the spirits he called upon were evil. Further, the power of the Devil is so overwhelming that anyone foolishly attempting to control his servants will find himself instead controlled by them. The sorcerer becomes the servant of the demons and a subject of Satan. The grounds for the transformation of sorcery into witchcraft had been fully prepared.

After the Apocalyptic period, Satan's role in Judaism dwindled, since the Rabbis, who dominated Judaism from the first century onwards, gave him little attention. But Christianity was founded in the midst of the Apocalyptic period, and in consequence the New Testament and subsequent Christian thought have given Satan a considerable role. The function of the Devil in the New Testament is as counterprinciple to Christ. The central message of the New Testament is that Christ saves us. What he saves us from is the power of the Devil. The opposition between the Lord and the Devil is fierce and profound, and any who stand in the Saviour's way or attempt to frustrate his plan of salvation are either explicitly or implicitly servants of Satan. The Devil has under his supreme command all opposition to the Lord both natural and supernatural, including demons, infidels, heretics, and sorcerers. The early Christians had a particular distaste for sorcerers. Claiming that the wonders worked by Christ were evidence of his divine mission, the Christians were obliged to attack claims of similar wonders performed by sorcerers as spurious. Their own enemies, such as the pagan Celsus, dismissed Christianity by claiming that Christ was merely another sorcerer. Thus the Christians perceived sorcery as both an insult and a threat.

The Christian attitude towards sorcerers was clear from the Books of Acts onwards. When Paul and Barnabas visited Paphos they found there 'a certain sorcerer, a false prophet' named Barjesus or Elymas. Elymas sought to turn the apostles away from the faith, and Paul, filled with the Holy Spirit, cursed him: 'O full of all subtlety and mischief, thou child of the Devil, thou enemy of all righteousness . . . the hand of the Lord is upon thee, and thou shalt be blind, not seeing the sun for a season' (Acts 13:6–12). Simon the *magos*, whose conversion and baptism are recorded in Acts 8:9–13, became in later Christian tradition one of the prototypes of the diabolical sorcerer. The stance of Christianity was clear. On the one hand there were the followers of goodness and light, on the other, the minions of evil and darkness, among whom the sorcerers were prominent. Sorcery had come a long way from its origins in simple, mechanical magic.

2 The roots of European witchcraft

A strange picture of witchcraft was drawn by writers of the fifteenth and sixteenth centuries during the witch-craze.

The sun has gone down, and honest people are asleep. The witches, including some men but mostly women, creep silently out of their beds, making sure that they do not disturb their husbands or wives. They are preparing for the sabbat. Those who live near the meeting ground will go on foot; those who live farther away will go to a private place, rub their bodies with an ointment that enables them to levitate, and fly off on animals, fence-rails, brooms, or stools. At the meeting, which takes place in a cellar, cave, or deserted heath, they meet ten to twenty of their fellow witches. If a neophyte is there, an initiation ceremony precedes the ordinary business of the meeting. The novice will be bound to the cult in such a way that he or she will find it difficult to withdraw. Accordingly, she is obliged to swear to keep the secrets of the cult, and she further seals herself to the group by promising to kill a young child and bring its body to a subsequent meeting. She orally renounces the Christian faith and seals her apostasy by stamping on, or excreting on, a crucifix or a consecrated host. Next she adores the male master of the cult, the Devil or his representative, by offering him the obscene kiss on the buttocks.

When the initiation has been completed, the assembly takes part in feasting and drinking. The witches enact a parody of the eucharistic feast, bringing in the bodies of children whom they have previously murdered. The infants may be stolen from Christian families, or they may be the offspring conceived by the witches at previous orgies. The children are offered up in sacrifice to the Devil. The witches may boil the children's bodies, mix them with loathsome substances, and render them into the levitating ointment. Or they may consume the children's body and blood in ritual parody of the Lord's Supper.

After the feast the torches are extinguished, or the candelabras are overturned by a black dog or cat. The orgy commences. Cries of 'Mix it up' are heard, and each person takes the one next him in lascivious embrace. The encounters are indiscriminate: men with men, women with women, mothers with sons, brothers with sisters. When the orgy is concluded, the witches take ritual leave of their master and return home replete to join their sleeping spouses.

Such a scene never occurred, but this is what was almost universally believed to happen at a witch's sabbat. What people believe to be true influences their actions more than what is objectively true, and the conviction that this picture was accurate brought about the execution of hundreds of thousands of people. The charges on which these people were put to death

were at best distorted and exaggerated; at worst they were an invention and an imposture.

What are the origins of these beliefs and how did they come to be assembled? What social and psychological patterns produced and maintained these beliefs and their consequences? What is the significance of such behaviour for our understanding of human nature today? These are some of the questions that will be addressed in the following chapters.

What are the origins of these beliefs? The picture of witchcraft drawn above did not fully emerge before the fifteenth century. In the beginning, European sorcery was similar to that elsewhere in the world. The transformation was largely the result of the action of Christian thought upon pagan sorcery and religion. But Christianity did not conquer Europe overnight. Within the Roman Empire, conversion required four centuries from the birth of Christ to the establishment of Christianity by Theodosius. Beyond the northern boundaries of the Empire the process was not completed until the seventh century (England), ninth century (Germany), or even twelfth century (Scandinavia).

During this long period Christian theology gradually moved the transformation of sorcery along. Augustine, the most influential Christian theologian, argued that pagan magic, religion, and sorcery were all invented by the Devil for the purpose of luring humanity away from Christian truth. Some of the effects of sorcery are illusions, Augustine said; others are real. Both reality and illusion are works of the Devil. Sorcerers summoning up spirits are calling up demons. And now Christian theologians made another important identification: the demons that the sorcerers were calling up were the pagan gods. Jupiter, Diana, and the other deities of the Roman pantheon

Collin de Plancy, *The Sabbat.* This nineteenth-century panoramic view illustrates many of the clichés of witchcraft: the flight through the air, the use of sacrificed children in the preparation of the magical salve, the veneration of the Devil, the backward dance, and the revel.

Opposite: Goya, *The Witches' Kitchen, c.* 1794–5. The witches are using their magical salve to enable them to change their shapes and levitate on brooms.

39

An antler-headed Celtic god, a detail from the Gundestrup cauldron deposited as a votive offering in a Danish bog during the second or first century BC. Horns are a worldwide symbol of power, fertility, and plenitude of game.

were really demons, servants of Satan. As Christianity pressed northward, it made the same assertion about Wotan, Freya, and the other gods of the Celts and Teutons. Those who worshipped the gods worshipped demons whether they knew it or not. With this stroke, all pagans, as well as sorcerers, could be viewed as part of the monstrous plan of Satan to frustrate the salvation of the world. This was the posture of most theologians and church councils. Yet at the same time popular religion often treated the pagan deities quite differently, transferring the characteristics of the gods to the personalities of the saints. In modern Greece, or in modern Ireland, one can still find traces of the old gods in saints who bring storms, protect holy wells, or bellow out the thunder. In fact considerable differences existed between the religions of the Mediterranean and those of the north, but Christianity lumped them all together as 'pagan'. The term 'pagan', meaning 'hick' or 'bumpkin', was an opprobrious one that the Christians applied uncritically and without distinction to all the monist/polytheist religions they encountered.

The encounter between Christianity and Celtic and Teutonic religions was one of the most important steps in the formation of historical witchcraft. It is also a crucial point in the interpretation of witchcraft today.

INTERPRETATIONS OF EUROPEAN WITCHCRAFT

At least four major interpretations of European witchcraft are current. The first is the old liberal view that witchcraft never existed at all but was a monstrous invention by the ecclesiastical authorities in order to enhance their powers and enlarge their purses. For this school, the history of witchcraft is a chapter in the history of repression and inhumanity.

The second tradition is the folklorist or Murrayite tradition. Margaret Murray published her *Witch-Cult in Western Europe* in 1921, at a time when Sir James Frazer's *Golden Bough* and his ideas about fertility cults were dominating a whole generation of writers. Influenced by Frazer and by her own background as an Egyptologist, Murray argued that European witchcraft was an ancient fertility religion based on the worship of the horned god Dianus. This ancient religion, Murray claimed, had survived into the Middle Ages and at least into the early modern period. Murray was enshrined in fiction as Rose Lorimer in Angus Wilson's *Anglo-Saxon Attitudes*; the *Encyclopaedia Britannica* used her article on 'witchcraft' for decades; and a number of historians and folklorists followed her lead. In Germany, Anton Meyer argued a variant that was to become popular with modern witches: Meyer's view was that the ancient fertility religion emphasized the earth goddess more than the horned god.

Modern historical scholarship rejects the Murray thesis with all its variants. Scholars have gone too far in their retreat from Murray, since many fragments of pagan religion do certainly appear in medieval witchcraft. But the fact remains that the Murray thesis on the whole is untenable. The argument for the survival of any coherent fertility cult from antiquity through the Middle Ages into the present is riddled with fallacies:

(1) The original religion from which Murray asserted witchcraft derived was the religion of Dianus. This religion never existed; it is a composite artificially created by Miss Murray out of the characteristics of discrete and divergent religions from Asia Minor to Wales. Murray's argument verged on accepting the Christian polemic that all pagan religions are alike.

(2) Even if such a composite fertility religion had existed, evidence for its survival is wholly inadequate. Certainly paganism did not die out at the first trumpet of Christianity, and it lingered longer in some areas – such as Scandinavia and Russia – than others. But by the twelfth century virtually all of Europe had been converted. In every area, bits and pieces of pagan beliefs and practices survived the conversion and persisted through the Middle Ages. But no evidence exists that any organized pagan cult or theology existed in the Middle Ages. As Elliot Rose observed, 'Of course, many popular festivals . . . were survivals *from* paganism; this is not the same as a survival *of* paganism.' And 'in no single instance of all those [explanations] put forward by Miss Murray is there not an alternative and a better explanation of the facts.'[15]

(3) Not until about 1300, a thousand years after the conversion of Constantine, does a substantial body of evidence about witchcraft appear, and this evidence shows witchcraft not as a fertility religion but as a Christian heresy based upon diabolism. Whether this diabolical witchcraft actually existed or whether it was invented by the Christians, the Murrayite thesis fails. If witches *did* exist in the 1300–1700 period, all the evidence shows them as heretical diabolists, not pagans. If on the other hand the liberals are correct and witchcraft was an invention, then it did not exist at all. In either case the survival of an 'old religion' is out of the question.

(4) Two huge time gaps in the evidence exist. The first is the one from the conversion to the beginning of the witch-craze; the second extends from the

Figure with a horned helmet on an Anglo-Saxon bronze buckle from Finglesham in Kent. Such pagan images were later transformed into the idea of the Christian Devil.

end of the witch-craze to the time of Leland's *Aradia* at the end of the nineteenth century (see p. 148). In the late eighteenth and nineteenth centuries there is no evidence for the existence of witchcraft at all. Some isolated pagan practices, yes. Sorcery, yes. But neither witchcraft as diabolism nor witchcraft as 'the old religion'. That this 'old religion' persisted secretly, without leaving any evidence, is of course possible, just as it is possible that below the surface of the moon lie extensive deposits of Stilton cheese. Anything is possible. But it is nonsense to assert the existence of something for which no evidence exists. The Murrayites ask us to swallow a most peculiar sandwich: a large piece of the wrong evidence between two thick slices of no evidence at all.

A third school, currently the most influential, emphasizes the social history of witchcraft, especially the social pattern of witch accusations. These historians generally assume that witchcraft (as opposed to sorcery) never really existed, their difference with the old-fashioned liberals being that they blame belief in witchcraft on widespread general superstition rather than on the impostures of an evil Church. A fourth group of historians emphasizes the history of ideas and argues that witchcraft is a composite of concepts gradually assembled over the centuries. Of these, Christian heresy and theology are more important than paganism. Both these groups have ignored or dismissed modern witchcraft. This book takes both historical witchcraft and modern witchcraft into account but treats them as separate phenomena with no historical connection between them.

SORCERY, FOLKLORE, AND RELIGION IN PAGAN EUROPE

The roots of historical European witchcraft lie partly in Graeco-Roman and Hebrew thought and partly in the sorcery, folklore and religion of northern Europe. The Bronze Age sorcery of northern Europe was of a piece with sorcery all over the world: a burial site reveals a Bronze Age woman, possibly a sorceress, buried with the claw-joint of a lynx, the bones of a weasel, spinal joints of snakes, horses' teeth, a rowan twig, a broken knife blade, and two pieces of iron pyrites, all of which were apparently believed to possess magical qualities. The almost total lack of sources prohibits any investigation of the course of sorcery from the Bronze Age to the time of conversion, and the vast cultural shifts and differences rule out the likelihood of any coherent tradition. Yet the folk-sorcery of the early Christian period in the north is still, like that of the Bronze Age, common sorcery.

The Norsemen raised evil spirits and destroyed the spiritual protection of an enemy by placing a horse's head with its mouth open on a pole in front of his house. Teutonic sorcerers used herbs, sieves, and figures of wax, dough, or lime in their work. In hostile magic, they took the figure and hung it up in the air, plunged it in water, heated it at the fire, or stabbed it with needles. Charms were used to hurt or heal. A simple charm that persisted into the nineteenth century was: *Sprach jungfrau Hille/blut stand stille*, 'The maiden Hille has spoken/the flow of blood is checked'. The charm illustrates the survival of pagan elements long after the extinction of paganism. The maid Hille is the ancient Valkyr Hilda, but the modern peasant mumbling the

Opposite: detail of Shetelig's sledge from the ninth-century Oseberg ship burial. Such grotesques, used by the Norsemen to frighten human or supernatural enemies, entered into the iconography of the Devil and his demons.

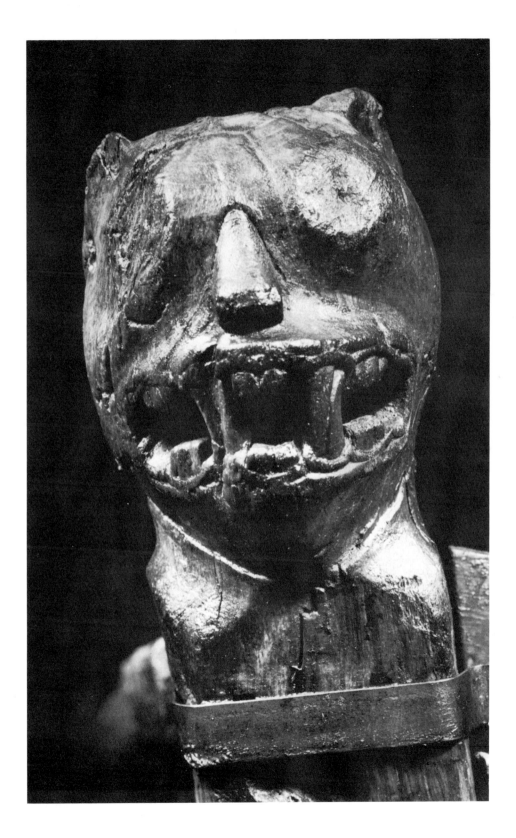

charm was no more a pagan than the modern Italian who a generation ago used the exclamation *perbacco*, 'by Bacchus'. Many individuals today shout 'Jesus Christ' or 'God damn it' without either hope of salvation or fear of damnation.

To destroy an enemy, the Anglo-Saxons recited a spell reducing him to nothing by associating him with tiny and perishable things in nature:

> May you be consumed as coal upon the hearth,
> May you shrink as dung upon a wall,
> and may you dry up as water in a pail.
> May you become as small as a linseed grain,
> and much smaller than the hipbone of an itchmite,
> and may you become so small that you become nothing.

Some Anglo-Saxon magic was simple and mechanical:

Against warts. Take the water of a dog and the blood of a mouse, mix together, smear the warts with this; they will soon disappear.

Sometimes the curse mingled mechanical with religious elements:

If a man is troubled by tumours near the heart, let a girl go to a spring that runs due east, and let her draw a cupful of water moving with the current, and let her sing on it the Creed and an Our Father.

Or:

A pleasant drink against insanity. Put in ale hassock, lupine, carrot, fennel, radish, betony, water-agrimony, marche, rue, wormwood, cat's mint, elecampane, enchanter's nightshade, wild teazle. Sing twelve Masses over the drink, and let the patient drink it. He will soon be better.[16]

Christian penitentials, guides for priests in the early Middle Ages for use in hearing confessions and assigning penances, condemn customs derived from ancient sorcery. These customs, whatever their original rationales, had become superstitions, since they now lacked any integrating or coherent world view. 'If any woman', prescribed the penitential of Theodore about AD 600,

puts her daughter upon a roof or into an oven for the cure of a fever, she shall do penance for seven years.

The unconscious symbolism of this particular spell is universal, at least as regards the oven. An oven, like a cave, represents the womb: passing a child into an oven and bringing it out again symbolizes rebirth. In sorcery, the symbol becomes a part of the occult system of interconnections and produces a physical cure. The Christian authorities viewed all such work as being effected by the intervention of demons and sought to repress it. The Confessional of Egbert (about 750) decrees:

If a woman works [sorcery] (*drycraeft*) and enchantment (*galdor*) and [uses] magical philters, she shall fast for twelve months. . . . If she kills anyone by her philters, she shall fast for seven years.[17]

The Norse *Edda* says that *seithr* (sorcery) was performed at night, when men are asleep, by *völvas* (sorceresses) who rode out at night on boars, wolves,

Opposite: an Anglo-Saxon magician. Early medieval sorcerers were not accused of diabolism. However, it was usually assumed that the practice of sorcery involved calling up and employing spirits. As in this eleventh-century picture, the sorcerer sometimes got more than he bargained for.

Witches making rain, a woodcut of 1489. Weather-magic is a form of sorcery found all over the world. Destructive weather-magic, together with magic causing other natural disasters such as famines or infestations of locusts, was during the witch-craze included among the *maleficia* or evil deeds thought to be performed by witches.

Opposite: Diana. Roman goddess of the hunt and protectress of animals, Diana was associated with witchcraft as a night goddess, a goddess of the underworld (in her form of Hecate), and as a leader of the Wild Hunt or wild rout of witches.

or fence-rails to meet their fellow-sorcerers at the *trolla-thing* or spirit meeting. 'Ketill was roused at night', the *Edda* relates,

by a great uproar in the wood; he ran out and saw a sorceress with streaming hair; being questioned, she begged him not to balk her, [for] she was bound for a magic [meeting], to which were coming Skelking king of spirits from Dumbshaf [and other spirits].

Christians of course interpreted such a meeting as a diabolical 'sabbat'.

Peasants often practised sorcery in order to improve their own position at the expense of their neighbours, or simply to exercise their spite. Sometimes the threat of a hex could be lucrative. Visigothic laws of the sixth century prescribed whipping as punishment for self-advertised 'storm-makers' who made farmers pay them to spare their fields. Many of the charges of evil magic common during the witch-craze were of such ancient origin: making storms, causing death or disease in animals or humans, and producing impotence.

Folk-tales about witchcraft and sorcery generally reflect both a fear of sorcerers and a sense of their power. The 'witch' of the folk-tale is basically a sorcerer (rarely do charges derived from the witch-craze enter into folk-tales). She is closely associated with the powers of nature and has many of the aspects of a nature spirit herself. She is close to the 'woodwives' or 'wild women' of folklore who represent the wildness of nature as opposed to the world of civilized humanity. Here is a common motif:

A girl becomes the servant of a black witch in the woods. There is a forbidden chamber . . . into which she may not go. She has to clean the house for many years. . . . She eventually opens the door of the secret forbidden chamber and finds in it the black witch who, through her cleaning, has already turned nearly white. The girl shuts up the room again but is then persecuted by the witch for having transgressed the taboo. [The witch] persecutes the girl, takes away her children and brings every kind of misery over her, [compelling her to lie and say that she has not seen her in the chamber].[18]

Folk-tales, like dreams, express the concerns of the unconscious in symbols; the meaning of the figure of the witch, like the meaning of any symbol, varies with the story. Usually, however, she represents an elemental natural force possessing enormous and unexpected powers against which a natural person is unable to prepare or defend himself, a force not necessarily evil, but so alien and remote from the world of mankind as to constitute a threat to the social, ethical, and even physical order of the cosmos. This manner of portraying the witch is very ancient and probably archetypal. This witch is neither a simple sorceress, nor a demonolater, nor a pagan. She is a hostile presence from another world. The gut terror inspired by this archetypal witch helps to explain the excesses of hatred and fear that welled up during the witch-craze.

Sometimes Celtic and Teutonic traditions merged with those of Greece and Rome. The Roman goddess Diana, for example, blended with the Teutonic fertility goddesses in the early Middle Ages. Diana was goddess of the moon, virgin huntress, and heavenly sister of the sun-god Apollo. But Diana was not always light and airy. Her association with animals made her

Hecate, a form of Diana, was a goddess whose three faces represented power over the underworld, earth, and air. She was also associated with night and with malevolent magic. The three faces of Hecate are one source for Dante's idea that Satan has three faces in hell.

a feral protectress of animals as well as a huntress, and her function of assuring plenitude of game connected her with fertility in general. Her power over the moon associated her with the monthly cycles of human females; and the horns of the crescent moon, symbolizing growth, reinforced the element of fertility.

Since the underworld both pushes up the new crops to the light and swallows them up when they die and rot, fertility deities are also associated with death, and Diana was identified with three-faced Hecate, dread pale goddess of death, patroness of evil sorcery, and mother of lamias. In this dark form, Diana appeared in early medieval belief as a leader of witch processions and rites. But the origins of these Dianic processions, unknown in Rome, are more Teutonic than Mediterranean and have their roots in the Wild Hunt.

A Wild Man and Woman, by
Jean Bourdichon, fifteenth
century. The legendary wild
people of the medieval forests
were sometimes associated
with the Wild Hunt and
with witchcraft.

The Wild Hunt was a procession of spirits or ghosts who roamed through
the countryside revelling and destroying. The leader of this ghastly rout was
sometimes female, sometimes male. The female leader was in northern
Germany called Holda, Holle, or Holt, 'the friendly one', wife of Wotan,
goddess of marriage and fecundity; in the south she was called Perchta,
Berhta, or Berta, 'the bright one'. This goddess was associated through the
hunt, the moon, and the night, with Diana. The association was probably
made in the minds of scholars and churchmen who applied a familiar
classical name, Diana, to the unfamiliar goddess of the Teutons. An even
more curious connection was made between Berta/Holda and Herodias, the
murderous wife of Herod: the dark reputation of Herodias and the *Her*-
element in her name seem to have caused the association. When the leader of

the Wild Hunt was male, his name too began with *Ber-* or *Her-* (Berthold, Herlechin, or Herne), relating him to brightness and the cult of the moon.

The members of the Wild Hunt roamed the wilderness, the heaths, and the forests. They were akin to the 'wild men and women' who, part human, part animal, and part spirit, were believed to roam the medieval forests. Elements of the wild woman, often perceived as a murderess, child-eater, and bloodsucker, lingered in the folk-tales of the lonely witch who dwelt in the forest: gradually in the early Middle Ages the characteristics of the wild huntresses and wild women were transferred to the witches.

Nothing persists in the mind more than the memory of a holiday, and traces of ancient pagan festivals can be clearly found in the Middle Ages and down to the present. Some of the pagan festivals are still (though now in the late twentieth century self-consciously) practised in small towns and villages in the British Isles, Germany, and elsewhere in Europe. Some of the more important festivals acquired a sinister reputation and came to be associated during the witch-craze with the meetings or 'sabbats' of witches. Contemporary witches, drawing proudly on both the ancient festivals themselves and their association with medieval and early modern witches, have made these ancient feasts the foundation of their own major 'sabbats'.

During the witch-craze, five festivals most frequently appear in the sources. The first was 31 October. The purpose of the original pagan rite on this day was to restore the power of the waning sun. Among the Anglo-Saxons this rite was called the 'need-fire', because great bonfires were kindled to lend strength to the sun through imitative magic. When the Christians established 1 November as All Saints' Day or All Hallows' Day, the need-fire festival fell on All Hallows' Eve and was transformed into Hallowe'en. In England, this religious displacement of the holiday was followed in the seventeenth century by a political displacement. After the arrest of Guy Fawkes for plotting to blow up Parliament, the date of his apprehension, 5 November, became a national holiday. On that day bonfires are still lit and rockets set off. In America, Hallowe'en became a kind of Saturnalia for children, a night when the rules were suspended for a while and children ventured out, like elves, to demand treats and threaten reprisals against the stingy. It has since become commercialized, but still the memory of strange spirits and weird fires lingers.

Another festival designed to bring back the sun and insure fertility was practised about the time of the winter solstice, and in the early Middle Ages some people were still dressing as stags and bulls on 1 January and performing a ritual dance to insure the plenitude of game. Another fire festival, later associated with the Christian feast of Candlemas, was celebrated about 1 February. Another occurred on 30 April, the eve of May Day, which has always been a common date for the celebration of the return of spring. 30 April happened by chance to become the Christian feast of an obscure Anglo-Saxon missionary named St Walpurga, and from this coincidence derives the name Walpurgisnacht or Walpurgisnight. Then, on 30 June, Midsummer's Eve, the return of the sun and the bounty of summer were celebrated. *A Midsummer Night's Dream* preserves the magical atmosphere of this festival.

Palaeolithic cave-drawing of a stag or dancer in a stag costume. Dances in which people wore animal clothes to secure plenty of game were practised for millennia in Europe and may have been one origin of the idea of shape-shifting. The stag dances held annually on 1 January were condemned by the Christian Church and associated with witchcraft.

Herne the Hunter, by George Cruikshank, 1843. Herne was one form of the mysterious and deadly leader of the Wild Hunt; he was often associated with the Devil.

Mrs Samuel conjuring up the Devil. An illustration to an account of the witch trial of 1593 at Warboys in Huntingdonshire. The witch, standing within her protective circle, summons the Devil and her familiars, the spirits of evil.

The familiars of later witches originated with the dwarves, fairies, trolls, kobolds, or other small spirits of northern folklore. They could be friendly, mischievous, or malignant. In origin they were nature spirits, but Christianity could admit the existence of no spiritual entities other than God, angels, and demons. The Church equated these spirits with minor demons and took the association of the sorcerer with the familiar spirit as another sign of his relationship with the Devil. Yet the origin of the familiars in folklore rather than in demonology appears in the names assigned them, names such as Robin Goodfellow, Haussibut, Federwisch, or Rumpelstilt-skin. Such spirits are to be found in cabbage rows or behind larch boughs rather than in the serried ranks of Satan's hell.

THE LEGAL STATUS OF SORCERY

All survivals of pagan belief, worship, and practice were condemned as demonic and gradually suppressed by Christian theology and law. Roman law had been stern in dealing with sorcery. Teutonic law was much milder. But in the course of the eighth and ninth centuries the growing influence of theology upon civil law produced a legal association of sorcerers with demons. The word *maleficium*, originally 'wrongdoing' in general, now came to mean malevolent sorcery in particular, and the *maleficus* or *malefica* was presumed to be closely associated with the Devil. Sorcery could now be prosecuted not simply as a crime against society but as a heresy and a crime against God.

The law fixed the identification of paganism with demonolatry. A 'List of Superstitions' drawn up at the Council of Leptinnes in 744 prohibited sacrifice to saints, evidence of the lingering confusion in the popular mind between new saint and old deity. The same council approved a baptismal formula that asked the catechumen to 'renounce all the works of the demon, and all his words, and Thor, and Odin, and Saxnot, and all evil beings that are like them.' Charlemagne ordered death for anyone sacrificing 'a human being to the Devil and [offering] sacrifice to demons as is the custom of the pagans.'[19]

The law helped transfer the characteristics of evil spirits to human witches. The pagans had set out offerings of food and drink for minor spirits. The Synod of Rome in 743 assumed that these spirits were demons and outlawed the offerings. The demonic spirits were then transformed into *bonae mulieres*, the ghostly 'good women' who wandered out at night going into houses and stealing food. Finally, the *bonae mulieres* were transformed into witches. Likewise, the term *striga* or *stria*, originally a blood-drinking night spirit, became a common word for a witch.

The early Middle Ages were tolerant of sorcery and heresy in comparison with the tortures and executions of the Roman Empire and with the hangings and burnings of the later Middle Ages and Renaissance. Two or three years' penance was normal for *maleficium*, incantation, and idolatry. But the law gradually became both more comprehensive and more severe. The Synod of Paris on 6 June 829 issued a decree with sinister implications for the future, citing the stern passages of Leviticus 20:6 and Exodus 22:18. The synod argued that since the Bible decreed that a *maleficus* should not be permitted to live, the king had a right to punish sorcerers severely. In England Alfred the Great threatened *wiccan* with the death penalty, and Ethelstan ordered execution for *wiccecraeft* if it resulted in death.

Such measures were bound to reduce and eventually eradicate pagan practices, and condemnations of pagan rites gradually became perfunctory repetitions of earlier condemnations issued when the problem was more serious. Once in a while the sources report something fresh, such as the struggle of St Barbato against the residual paganism of the Lombards in the ninth century. At Benevento these pagans adored a snake and a sacred tree, around which they danced in a circle. The Synod of Rome in 826 complained that 'many people, mostly women, come to Church on Sundays and holy days not to attend the Mass but to dance, sing broad songs, and do other such pagan things.'[20]

The most important legal document of the early Middle Ages relating to witchcraft is the Canon Episcopi, issued about AD 900. The canon says:

Some wicked women are perverted by the Devil and led astray by illusions and fantasies induced by demons, so that they believe that they ride out at night on beasts with Diana, the pagan goddess, and a horde of women. They believe that in the silence of the night they cross huge distances. They say that they obey Diana's commands and on certain nights are called out in her service. . . . Many other people also believe this to be true, although it is a pagan error to believe that any other divinity exists than the one God. . . . Such fantasies are thrust into the minds of faithless people, not by God, but by the Devil. For Satan has the power to transform himself into the figure of an angel of light. In this form he captures and enslaves the mind of a miserable woman and transforms himself into the shapes of various different people. He shows her deluded mind strange things and unknown people, and leads it on weird journeys. It is only the mind that does this, but faithless people believe that these things happen to the body as well.[21]

The Canon Episcopi had enormous influence. It was widely and incorrectly believed to date back to the fourth century and, thus possessing the authority of great antiquity, entered into the major medieval collections of canon law. Since the canon dismissed the physical reality of witchcraft and condemned those who believed in it as weak in faith, it helped to forestall the witch-craze. Later, when canon lawyers and theologians accepted the reality of witchcraft, they had to twist and bend their way around the canon. Yet the Canon Episcopi is far from a monument to early medieval scepticism, for it indicates that belief in these strange phenomena was widespread, and its influence helped to spread them. The Canon Episcopi itself helped establish the historical concept of the sabbat. As the chief of a demon horde, Diana was equated with Satan. The women who followed her must then be worshippers of the Devil. Though they did not really follow her out in their physical bodies, they did ride with her in spirit, so that their spirits were servants of Satan. They obeyed the Lady goddess (*domina*) rather than the Lord Christ (*dominus*), and they met secretly on specified nights to worship her. A century later, the canon lawyer Burchard of Worms equated the Diana of the Canon with Holda, whom he called 'the witch Holda'. The Classical goddess Diana had been identified with the Teutonic mother-goddess Holda, and both had been judged to be manifestations of Satan. The ambivalent identification of Holda as a witch, together with the image of the women who followed her out at night, created a picture on which the witch-craze would later draw extensively.

3 Witchcraft, heresy, and inquisition

Sorcery, pagan religion, and folklore were the first three elements in the formation of European witchcraft. Christian heresy was the fourth. When the witch-craze began at the end of the Middle Ages, its most important beliefs were: (1) the ride by night, (2) the pact with the Devil, (3) the formal repudiation of Christianity, (4) the secret, nocturnal meeting, (5) the desecration of the eucharist and the crucifix, (6) the orgy, (7) sacrificial infanticide, and (8) cannibalism. Every one of these elements was either introduced into the tradition of witchcraft by heresy or at least heavily modified by it.

The idea of pact was crucial, because it put the cap on the demonization of the sorcerer. A *maleficus* was now by definition one who makes a pact with Satan. Pact helped distinguish witchcraft from possession. The Devil may possess a person against his will, but pact is always voluntary. The witch, then, serves the Devil of her own free will. The idea of pact began to gain currency in the eighth century, when Paul the Deacon, one of Charlemagne's advisers, translated a sixth-century Greek story about a priest named Theophilus who obtained promotion to the episcopate by solemnly promising the Devil to renounce Christ. The motif of pact in medieval legend culminated in the story of Faust, the fictional high magician of the Renaissance who made a pact with the Devil to obtain both wisdom and sensual delight. The legend mingled the traditions of high and low magic and remained popular for centuries, witness Marlowe's *Dr Faustus* of the sixteenth century and Goethe's *Faust* of the nineteenth.

A typical story was told by Archbishop Hincmar of Reims in 860. A young man went to a sorcerer in order to procure the favours of a young girl. The sorcerer agreed to help him but on the condition that he renounce Christ in writing. The boy agreed, and the sorcerer wrote the Devil a letter expressing his hope that the dark lord would be pleased with his new recruit. The sorcerer handed the letter to the young man and told him to go out at night and hold the letter up in the air. That very night the boy went out, lifted up the letter, and called upon Satan for help. The Prince of Power of the Shadows appeared and led him into the presence of Satan, who examined the boy in a parody of the rite of baptism. 'Do you believe in me?' the Devil asked. 'I believe,' the boy replied. 'Do you renounce Christ?' 'I do renounce him.' 'You Christians always come to me when you need help and then try to repent afterwards, relying upon the mercy of Christ. I want you to promise yourself to me in writing so that there will be no possibility of escape.'

Pact with the Devil. The witches, protected by their circle, have called up Satan, who approaches them to offer his services in return for their souls. This idea of formal pact was the centrepiece of the inquisitors' prosecution of witches.

The Story of Theophilus, from the Ingeborg Psalter (before 1210). The story dates back to the sixth century and is the first account of a formal pact with the Devil. In this picture, Theophilus does feudal homage to his new master, who holds the written contract.

The Tragicall Hiſtoy of the Life and Death

of Doctor Fauſtus.

With new Additions.

Written by *Ch. Mar. K*

LONDON,
Printed for *Iohn Wright*, and are to be ſold at his ſhop without
Newgate, at the ſigne of the Bible. 1620.

Frontispiece to the first edition of Christopher Marlowe's *Dr Faustus*, 1620. Faust, shown here protected by his magic circle while he conjures up the Devil, mixed high and low magic in his search for both knowledge and sensual delight.

57

The boy agreed, and the Devil in return caused the girl to fall in love with him. She asked her father to give her to the boy in marriage, but her father refused, as he wished her to enter a convent. The girl realized that she was under the power of demons but was unable to resist; she told her father that she would die unless she married the young man. But the boy could continue the imposture no longer and confessed. By the intervention of St Basil the girl was released from Satan's grip and went demurely into the nunnery; the boy turned to a good Christian life. The story is a typical *exemplum*, a moral tale designed for use in sermons.

Pact did not remain in the world of story. It was the basis of the transformation of the sorcerer into the heretic. If you worshipped Satan, it followed that you believed that Satan could save you from the justice of God, which is heresy; if you renounced Christ as your lord and put Satanism in his place, this was the most despicable and dangerous of all heresies.

The earliest heresies of the Middle Ages were far from diabolical; most of them were characterized instead by a zealous desire for the moral reform of the Church. But as early as the eighth century some elements of witchcraft began to appear in heresy, or at least in what people believed about heresy. Then, in 1022, one event linked heresy and witchcraft decisively.

THE DUALIST HERESIES

In 1022 King Robert of France presided over the first execution for heresy in the Middle Ages. During the trial a vast mob assembled outside the episcopal palace at Orleans and was barely restrained from lynching the heretics before they could be formally condemned and burnt. The events of 1022 at Orleans are noteworthy. First, after several centuries in which reports of heresy were sparse, a sizable group of heretics appeared in northern France without any antecedents. Second, their trial attracted the attention of the king and queen. Third, a vast crowd of ordinary people were so incensed by the heresy that they tried to murder the defendants. Fourth, the heretics were alleged to believe doctrines tinged with dualism to a degree unheard of in Western Europe for four hundred years – the ancient cosmic conflict between light and darkness, spirit and flesh, good and evil, had reappeared. Finally the heretics were accused of beliefs and practices that for the first time closely resembled those alleged of the witches at the height of the witch-craze. Whether any of the charges were valid, the core ideas of historical witchcraft were now assembled for the first time at a trial for heresy.

The Orleans heretics were accused of holding sex orgies at night in a secret place, either underground or in an abandoned building. The members of the group appeared bearing torches. Holding the torches, they chanted the names of demons until an evil spirit appeared. Now the lights were extinguished, and everyone seized the person closest to him in sexual embrace, whether mother, sister, or nun. The children conceived at the orgies were burned eight days after birth (a grotesque echo of Christian baptismal practice), and their ashes were confected in a substance that was then used in a blasphemous parody of holy communion.

The heretics were accused of believing that when filled with the Holy Spirit they had angelic visions and were transported without lapse of time from place to place. They adored the Devil and paid him homage; he appeared to them in the form of a beast, an angel of light, or a black man. They recited a litany of demons. They formally renounced Christ and desecrated the crucifix.

Of these witch charges the most significant are the sexual orgies, the sacrifice of human beings, specifically children, and cannibalism. These charges are all ancient. The Syrians brought them against the Jews, the Romans against the Christians, and the Christians against the Gnostics. Now they were being brought against the medieval heretics. A long succession of heresy trials drew upon the Orleans charges, and by the fourteenth and fifteenth centuries licentious and orgiastic excesses were so frequently alleged against the heretics that the transition from the prosecution of heresy to the witch-craze was made almost without difficulty. The reason that these ancient charges came to light again at Orleans in 1022 is that the Orleans heretics were accused of holding doctrines tinged with dualism. Not all the early heretics had been accused by the Christians of orgy and other ritual crimes. Only the Gnostics, the inheritors of religious dualism, were so

The ritual murder of children, often accompanied by cannibalism, was one of the most common charges levelled against the witches. If the children were not eaten, they were often supposed to have been boiled in a cauldron and their fat used to help confect the magical salve.

stigmatized. When Gnosticism died out, the charges disappeared. Now the return of dualism to European heresy revived and developed the charges until they became a central part of heresy and witchcraft.

Extreme dualism had begun in ancient Iran, as we have seen (p. 33 above), passed on to the Gnostics and Manicheans, and entered the Balkans, where it became the basis of the religion of the Bulgarian Bogomils. But Christianity itself was a semi-dualist religion, and in their zeal for reform and spiritual purity the heresies of the eleventh and twelfth centuries exaggerated the dualism inherent in Christianity to the point that their views appeared Gnostic to the orthodox. Thus when the orthodox condemned the heretics of Orleans they applied to them terms similar to those the Church fathers had used against the Gnostics.

Then, more than a century after Orleans, the Bogomils sent missionaries to Western Europe. Beginning in the 1140s, Bogomil ideas united with the dualism inherent in already existing heresy to produce a new heresy called Catharism, 'the religion of the pure'. Catharism was a strongly dualist religion, in that it strongly emphasized the power of the Devil in the world. The Catharists taught that the Spirit of Evil, the Devil, created the material world for the purpose of entrapping spirit in matter. He imprisoned the human soul in a cage of flesh. Since the God of the Old Testament created the material world, he is the Spirit of Evil. The true God, the God of goodness and light, is hidden and remote from this world. All the personages of the Old Testament are demon followers of the Spirit of Evil and darkness who rules the world. Christ was a pure spirit sent down by the good, hidden God in order to teach humanity how to escape from the matter that confined them. Since matter is evil, Christ was pure spirit, his body an illusion; he was not truly a man. Being pure spirit, he did not truly suffer on the cross, and the cross is to be despised as a symbol of a lie. The worst sin is procreation, since conception imprisons another individual spirit in the flesh. The Catholic Church was established by the Devil in order to delude people, but an individual may free himself from the bondage of matter by following the teachings of Catharism.

The Catharist emphasis upon the Devil influenced orthodox theology, so that the Devil came to play a much larger role in late medieval thought than he had earlier. Fear of the Devil's powers was one of the chief ingredients of the witch-craze. But the Catharist Devil had a curious influence of another kind as well. The Catharists emphasized the power of the Devil, not to serve him, but to fight him. Yet their insistence upon his power as Lord of this World contained the seed of a curious misinterpretation. If the Devil really has powers nearly equal to the Lord's, and if the true God of light is distant and hidden, and if the Devil presides over wealth, fame, sex, and other earthly delights, some might prefer to worship the deity that gave them access to such pleasures. This kind of thinking, twisted from a Catharist as well as from a Catholic point of view, may have emerged from a zealous but faulty grasp of Catharist doctrine. Evidence that this occurred comes from fourteenth-century Italy, where heretics believed that the Devil created the material world. Since the Devil was the creator of the world, he was more powerful than God, and should be worshipped in his place.[22]

The execution of two
Cathars: *Auto-da-fé*, by P.
Berruguete. Catharism
strongly emphasized the
power of the Devil in the
world. It paved the way for
the assimilation of heresy to
witchcraft in the popular
imagination.

The pronounced dualism of the Catharists also left them open to the same charges of cannibalism, infanticide, and orgy that had already been brought against the much less dualist heretics of Orleans. Though on the whole the Catharists were wholly innocent of such charges, it is possible that some may have been guilty. It is clear that some of the Gnostics of the second and third centuries AD (the Barbelognostics for example) did engage in such practices. The union of the ascetic with the licentious, of disgust for matter with indulgence of matter, is a strong theme in dualistic Gnosticism, which developed at least five doctrinal reasons for negating sexual and other morality: (1) the flesh must do service to the flesh before it can be overcome; (2) the body, being evil, should be degraded by obscene practices; (3) once we are filled with the Holy Spirit we can do no wrong, and the laws of this world do not apply to us; (4) those who are not filled with the Spirit may as well sin, since nothing can save them anyway; (5) true freedom and life in the Spirit requires the destruction of law. These Gnostic arguments were all available to the medieval Catharists.

If some Gnostics practised libertinism, most did not, and the evidence that Catharists practised it is all biased and suspect. Catharist doctrines and practices were open to such antinomian interpretations, but it is not clear that libertinism really was a serious problem with the Catharists. What is clear, however, is that the orthodox thought that it was and assumed that such practices took place on a large scale. Again, what people believed to happen was more important than what really happened, and the widespread belief in the libertinism of the heretics helped to shape the witch-craze. Alan of Lille, writing towards the turn of the thirteenth century, reported that the heretics argued that a person must practise promiscuity in order to free himself from attachment to all things earthly and diabolical. Alan's contemporary, Walter Map, said that the heretics engaged in obscene rites. Map's description of 1182 uses the word 'synagogue' to describe the meeting for the first time. This usage, obviously designed to spite the Jews, was common throughout the Middle Ages, being replaced only towards the end of the fifteenth century by the equally anti-Jewish term 'sabbat'. Here is what Map thought happened at the assembly:

About the first watch of the night, when gates, doors, and windows have been closed, the groups sit waiting in silence in their respective synagogues, and a black cat of marvelous size climbs down a rope which hangs in their midst. On seeing it, they put out the lights. They do not sing hymns or repeat them distinctly, but hum through clenched teeth and pantingly feel their way toward the place where they see their lord. When they have found him they kiss him, each the more humbly as he is the more inflamed by frenzy – some the feet, more under the tail, most the private parts.[23]

More than a hundred years before the witch-craze began, the paradigm of the witch's 'sabbat' was already clear in the accusations brought against the heretics. Such a description is inherently unlikely to be an accurate account of what the heretics did, or of what the witches would do. The history of European witchcraft is essentially the history of a concept whose relationship to physical reality was tenuous. And the concept took the lives of hundreds of thousands of people.

Another contribution of heresy to witchcraft is the idea that the witches met in groups. Sorcerers almost always practised magic singly, but heretics worked in communities. The Alpine Italian heretics of the fourteenth century met in assemblies of seven to forty-seven, with an average meeting of about twenty.[24] Once sorcery was transformed into heresy, the inquisitors assumed that the sorcerer-heretics, or witches, also practised in groups.

The *osculum infame* or 'obscene kiss', a ritual salute of the Devil's backside, was a typical accusation in the witch trials.

FROM SORCERY TO WITCHCRAFT

The gradual transformation from sorcery to witchcraft can be seen in popular beliefs as expressed in some stories of the twelfth and thirteenth centuries. William of Newburgh tells a tale about the reign of Henry I (1100–35). A country fellow was walking alone at night past an ancient burial mound. Looking around, he found a door hidden in the side of the mound and entered. Inside was a cave, brightly lit with lamps, where men and women were seated at a solemn banquet. One of them rose, invited the peasant in, and offered him a cup. The farmer pretended to drink but instead secretly poured out the liquid and then hid the cup under his clothing. Returning home, he found the cup to be of rich material and beautiful design, so he took it to King Henry, who gave him a reward. The feeling of this story is still very much the feeling of folklore: these are still fairy folk, not witches. Yet the feasting attributed to the fairies is close enough to the feasting attributed to the heretics to encourage assimilation.

William of Malmesbury tells the story of 'the witch of Berkeley' about 1142. In spite of her traditional name, the woman of Berkeley was still more a sorceress than a witch.

A woman living at Berkeley was a practitioner of sorcery and ancient divinations. She was a glutton and engaged in unbounded debaucheries, for she was not as yet an old woman. One day when she was feasting, a jackdaw, one of her favourites, set up a great commotion. When she heard his chattering, she dropped the knife from her hand, turned pale, and groaned: 'Today my plough has come to the end of its row; today I shall hear dreadful news.' [She later heard of the death of her son and his family. Discouraged, she turned her face to the wall to die. Calling her other children to her, she told them that she had lost her soul by practising diabolical arts and pleaded with them for help.] 'Although you cannot lift the sentence that has been passed on my soul, you may be able to save my body. Sew up my corpse in the skin of a stag, lay it on its back in a stone coffin; fasten the lid with lead and iron and lay upon it a stone bound round three times with a heavy chain; and let psalms be sung and masses said for fifty days.' [The children endeavoured to fulfil their dead mother's last wish, but] so heavy was the woman's guilt and so terrible the Devil's violence that their work and their prayers were in vain. For on the first two nights, while the choir of priests was singing psalms around the body, a band of demons smashed the bolt and forced their way through the door of the church. On the third night, towards dawn, the whole monastery was shaken to its foundations by the noise of the approaching enemy. One demon, who was taller and more terrible than the others, broke the gate to pieces. [He called the woman up from the coffin and dragged her out of the church, bearing her off screaming on a black horse.][25]

In the thirteenth century the tales bring the sorcerers ever closer to the Devil. Writing about 1214, Gervaise of Tilbury tells stories that he claims to have garnered from eye-witnesses. Men and women ride out at night over long distances. Certain people have seen their flight as they passed over land and sea. They are able to fly all over the globe, so long as none of them makes the mistake of uttering the name of Christ while in flight, for this will make them immediately fall and plunge to the ground. At Arles, Gervaise himself saw a woman who had thus been plunged into the Rhone and soaked as far as her navel. The witches enter people's houses in the course of these nocturnal journeys. They disturb sleepers by sitting on their chests and causing nightmares of suffocation and falling. They have sexual relations with sleeping men. They suck blood, steal infants from their beds, and rummage through baskets and bins for food. They take the form of cats, wolves, or other animals at will. Caesarius of Heisterbach, writing about 1220, tells of a knight of Liège who lost his money and was persuaded by one of his peasants to call up the Devil for financial assistance. The knight formally renounced God and rendered feudal homage to the Devil in exchange for the improvement of his fortunes. However, when the Devil went so far as to ask him to deny the Blessed Virgin, his chivalry rebelled, and he was saved by our grateful Lady's intervention.

To what extent are such tales popular legend and to what extent learned embroidery? Peasants did not write, so the stories we have are in the language of scholars. The change in emphasis from folklore and sorcery to diabolical witchcraft results in part from the influence of ancient literary tradition going back through the trials at Orleans to the early Church Fathers. The scholars' stories, widely circulated and preached as *exempla* from the pulpit, soon entered into popular culture, so that by the end of the thirteenth century both scholars and ordinary people were prepared to believe in the existence of a

The witch of Berkeley, having served the Devil as a sorceress during her lifetime, is carried off by the Devil from her tomb.

Christ defends the City of God against Satan. A twelfth-century illustration. Theologians began to stress the Devil's power as the chief of an army of demons who roamed the world, tempting people to sin.

Opposite: The Nightmare, by Henry Fuseli, 1781. A modern conception of the incubus, a demon who sexually abuses sleeping women. In witchcraft, the incubus had a slightly different function, as the witches voluntarily submitted to its embraces.

widespread witch-cult. This development was speeded by the growth of scholastic theology.

Theology was the fifth major element in the witch concept. Theological concern with the problem of the Devil had been increasing from the mid-twelfth century onwards, largely in response to the introduction of Catharism in the 1140s. Though rejecting the extreme dualism of the Catharists, Christian writers began to place greater emphasis upon the Devil's power as the chief of an army of demons who roamed the world actively attempting to undermine the saving mission of Christ and tempting people to sin. Renunciation of Christ and adoration of the Devil constituted the worst possible sin. The scholastic philosophy and theology that dominated Europe from the twelfth century onwards, though it brought few new elements to the concept of witchcraft, refined details, established rationales, and provided a coherent and authoritative intellectual structure that the witch-hunters could draw upon for support for their ideas.

Scholasticism emphasized the idea of pact. It also firmly established the idea of ritual intercourse between the witches and Satan. The ancient notion of orgy had the worshippers mingling sexually with one another. But the scholastics added to this tradition the notion of the incubus, the demonic

The Devil was usually thought of as male, so witches who submitted to him sexually were generally considered female.

spirit that has sexual intercourse with women, and so established the idea that at the sabbat the witches submitted sexually to their master Satan.

The scholastics firmly established the tradition that witches were more likely to be women than men. The master of the witch assembly was supposed to be, not an inferior demon, but the Devil himself, the prince and principle of evil. As an angel, the Devil was sexless, but also as an angel, he could take on either male or female form as he chose. But in theology, literature, and art, he almost invariably appeared as masculine. This is the result of an odd sexual bias. As the principle of evil and age-old adversary of the Lord, the Devil was a figure of great power, almost divinity. The Judaeo-Christian tradition was unable to attach such divinity to a female figure. Like God himself, then, the Devil was almost universally perceived as male. From this it followed that the Devil's sexual activity at the sabbat was that of a male, and though homosexuality was not precluded, he almost invariably cohabited with women. Hence the belief in the preponderance of women at the sabbat. Other suggestions as to the predominance of women have been made (see Chapter 6), but sexist religious assumptions are the most important reason. In the notorious *Malleus Maleficarum* of the late fifteenth century (see below, p. 79), sexism was explicit, Women, the *Malleus* claimed

to demonstrate at length, were more likely than men to be witches because they were weaker, more stupid, superstitious, and sensual.

Ideas introduced by the inquisitorial and other courts constitute the last major element in the concept of European witchcraft. In prosecuting the witches with the laws against heresy rather than with the laws against sorcery, the courts finalized the separation of witchcraft from sorcery. English law was an important exception, and witchcraft in England was always associated more with sorcery and less with heresy than on the continent. For this reason, English witches were hanged while their counterparts on the continent were burned: in England the crime of witchcraft was a civil crime, while on the continent it was a crime of religion.

From the twelfth century onwards both civil and canon law became gradually more severe in dealing with heresy. The authorities tightened their control over the courts, aided by the revival of Roman law with its centralized and systematic approach. Under Roman law, men and women were part of the corporation of the state and bound to conform to its principles. In the late Roman Empire, the codes of Theodosius and of Justinian had declared heresy lèse-majesté against God and hence at least as worthy of death as lèse-majesté against the emperor. The revival of such

In England, witches were prosecuted by the civil courts and hanged for their crimes; on the continent they were usually prosecuted by ecclesiastical courts and punished at the stake. (A: hangman; B: bellman; C: two sergeants; D: witchfinder taking money for his work.)

Roman concepts encouraged the imposition of much harsher penalties. Under their influence, German law codes of the thirteenth and fourteenth centuries commonly decreed death both for sorcerers and for relapsed heretics. As the laws tightened, they encouraged active searches for witches. Before the thirteenth century, individual personal accusation had been the only way of bringing a sorcerer to trial. But the bishops had initiated inquisitions – formal investigations – of their dioceses for heresy by the late twelfth century, and under the influence of Roman law the secular courts began to search out malefactors actively. When the authorities began actively seeking for culprits rather than passively waiting for accusations, the witch-craze had started.

Canon law was becoming stricter, partly under the influence of Roman law, partly because of the influence of the scholastic method in law, which called for careful organization and thoroughness. St Augustine had taught that error had no rights. St Thomas Aquinas insisted on the rights of the individual conscience but then went on to argue that heresy was a sin because such ignorance must be the result of criminal negligence. All pacts with demons, whether explicit or implicit, were tantamount to apostasy from the Christian faith, Aquinas argued, and this doctrine of 'implicit' pact became a favourite of the witch-hunters. In explicit pact, the individual would literally call up the Devil or a demon and enter into an agreement with him. In implicit pact, such an agreement was not necessary. Anyone who tenaciously professed heresy was assumed to have subjected himself to the Devil whether or not he had called him up, or intended to do so, or indeed even thought it was possible to do so. Under this doctrine all heretics, whatever their doctrines or intentions, were considered implicitly in league with Satan.

From the beginning of the eleventh century, burning was imposed on relapsed heretics with increasing frequency. In 1198 Pope Innocent III called for the execution of those who persisted in heresy after they had been punished by excommunication. As witchcraft was associated with heresy, the punishment of burning was extended to witches as well, and from the fifteenth century onwards, witches were treated even more severely than heretics, being burned on first conviction instead of upon relapse. As fear of heresy and witchcraft grew, torture, a feature of Roman rather than Germanic law, became common practice in Europe.

The inquisition was the most powerful agent in the enforcement of legal sanctions against heretics and witches. So long as heresy was only a minor threat, the Church left responsibility for the correction of dissent in the hands of the bishops. With the growth both of heresy and of ecclesiastical efficiency, the popes began to press for firmer measures. First the bishops were encouraged to expand their own 'inquisitions', and then, in the years between 1227 and 1235, the papal inquisition was established. The power of the inquisition was repeatedly corroborated by papal actions such as the bull *Ad Extirpanda* issued by Innocent IV in 1252, which authorized the seizure of heretics' goods and their imprisonment, torture and execution, all on minimal evidence.

The inquisition moved decisively to assimilate sorcery to heresy. The manuals for inquisitors that began to appear about 1230 often included

questions on witchcraft as well as on conventional heresy. In 1233 Pope Gregory IX accused the Waldensian heretics – really evangelical moralists – of attending assemblies where the Devil incarnate presided over orgies. Pope Alexander IV (1254–61) refused the request of the inquisition to give it jurisdiction over all sorcery, but he turned over to it all cases of sorcery that 'clearly involved heresy'. The inquisitors rapidly learned to use this loophole and to introduce charges of heresy into sorcery trials. The identification of sorcery with witchcraft had become a bureaucratic and legal convenience. Furthermore, conviction rates rose rapidly, because inquisitorial procedures were constructed in such a way as to make guilt easy to prove and innocence difficult to defend. The inquisitors were taught what to look for, and through examination, threats, and torture usually were able to find witchcraft wherever it existed, and wherever it did not. Each conviction crystallized the image of the witch more concretely in popular consciousness and established yet another precedent for generations of future inquisitors. The stage was now fully furnished for the opening of the great witch-craze.

The inquisition and other courts used a variety of torments to elicit confessions of witchcraft. Among the tortures shown here are the strappado, the rack, and the water torture.

4 The witch-craze on the continent of Europe

By 1300 all the elements of European witchcraft had been assembled. For the next century and a half fear of witches spread gradually throughout Europe. Then, about 1450, at the end of the Middle Ages, the fear became a craze which lasted more than two hundred years. The popular idea that the craze was medieval is the result of a false prejudice that links everything bad to the clericalism of the so-called 'Dark Ages'. Rather, the witch-craze was a product of the Renaissance and Reformation. Many of the intellectuals of the Renaissance and leaders of the Reformation were among the most forceful advocates of belief in diabolical witchcraft.

Some historians have attempted to treat the witch-craze in Europe as the anthropologists treat sorcery in Africa, and have looked for the function of witch beliefs in European society. But this approach has limitations. For one thing, European witchcraft is quite different from African sorcery; for another, the social and intellectual conditions of European witchcraft varied widely from area to area and period to period. It is possible to argue that witchcraft was a product of social anxiety and then link its beginnings with the social unrest of the fourteenth century and its plagues, famines, and wars. But that is too simple. Plagues, famines, and wars were endemic in the Middle Ages and early modern period. Every period in human history is troubled, but every period has not produced a witch-craze. Social explanations based more narrowly on local considerations help more, but then it remains difficult to explain why local outbreaks should have melded into a madness that engulfed almost the entire culture.

Historians have long debated the geographical origins of witchcraft. Josef Hansen, followed by Hugh Trevor-Roper, argued that witchcraft began in the mountains, where the thin air was conducive to hallucinations, severe natural phenomena such as storms and avalanches encouraged belief in demonic powers, and ancient sorceries lingered in benighted minds. The view is not wholly fair to mountain dwellers. In fact, witchcraft descended from heresy more than from sorcery and first appeared in the lowland cities where heresy was strong, only later spreading into the mountains where it gained strength from the lingering practices of ancient sorcery. Linked to the mountain theory is the idea that the Dominican inquisitors who led the attack on witchcraft in the fifteenth century generated witch beliefs by bringing into the mountains the unfamiliar social assumptions of the settled, feudal society of the lowlands. The generalization is too broad, but often the local church authorities did resist the inquisitors, and the intrusion of the Dominicans did generate tensions that promoted witch beliefs.

Psychology helps explain the craze. People projected evil desires and passions most easily upon isolated and lonely outsiders such as old widows and crones. Some of the accused, driven by fear and guilt, came to believe in their own guilt. The crazed nuns of Louviers and Loudun (see below, p. 88) believed that they made love with the Devil. The witch-craze is an important study in human evil, comparable to Nazism and Stalinism in the present century.

Legal sanctions against witchcraft grew steadily harsher as the notion grew that all sorcery involved pact with the Devil. The increasing harshness of legal theory was matched by the rising cruelty of legal practice. Each new conviction justified harsher measures, including torture; torture produced more confessions, confessions produced more convictions, and belief and repression fed one another.

A new intellectual ideology helped turn this vicious wheel. Many of the great Renaissance humanists were magicians. The Neoplatonism of these learned high magicians was quite different from the Aristotelianism that in scholastic circles encouraged the growth of witch beliefs.* Yet the rise of the witch-craze was concurrent with the rise of Renaissance magic. The humanists' belief in magic entailed belief in witchcraft, however much they took pains to insist that the wise and benevolent magic they practised was quite different from the evil magic of the witches. And this distinction was generally lost on public opinion, so that the result was that humanistic magic itself abetted the rise of the witch-craze.

Theologians and jurists agreed that witchcraft was the worst of heresies. In the early fifteenth century tracts dealing specifically with diabolical witchcraft began to appear. The scepticism and moderation that had characterized the medieval Canon Episcopi yielded more and more to belief that witchcraft was a sinister plot against the Church conceived and promoted by Satan himself. A learned debate on the reality of witchcraft continued between sceptics and believers, but after the publication of the *Malleus Maleficarum* in 1486 (see below, p. 79), the believers dominated for two centuries. 'It is rating our conjectures too highly to roast people alive for them,' the sceptic Montaigne exclaimed, but his was a minority voice. Ironically, the invention of the printing press in the 1450s at just the time that treatises on witchcraft were becoming common propagated the craze more rapidly. The invention of printing, like that of television later, did not necessarily promote wisdom or virtue.

At the beginning of the fourteenth century the old elements of folklore and heresy were still shaping witchcraft. In Austria a group of heretics were accused of worshipping Lucifer and believing that he would one day be restored to heaven while St Michael was cast into hell. On meeting, the heretics hailed one another with the words, 'May the injured Lucifer greet you'. They were supposed to have underground orgies, and one young woman was said to argue that she was a virgin above ground though sexually experienced under the earth. These Luciferans also preached doctrines similar

---

*Neoplatonism held that magic could be worked by natural means, Aristotelianism that all magic had to be done with the aid of spirits.

Ar leuue du diable
la mort print entre
ou monde . Et ce le
enfuiuent ceulx qui tiennent fo

to those of the Catharists and Waldensians. The Waldensians (*vaudois* in French) were actually reform-minded heretics, but so closely did the orthodox perceive the connection between witches and Waldensians that the witches were often called *vaudois*, and *aller en vauderie* came to mean 'to go to the witches' meeting'. The most common term for the meeting continued to be 'synagogue', though 'sabbat', equally insulting to Jews, became common in the next century.

Conrad Witz, *The Synagogue*, 1435. In a deliberate insult to Jews, Christian writers often referred to the witches' assembly as a 'synagogue'. Here the synagogue is represented as having been defeated by the Church: her staff of power is broken, and in her hands she clutches tablets on which mere gibberish is engraved. Jews and heretics, as well as witches, were viewed as helping Satan block Christ's work of salvation.

Opposite: Waldensian heretics. Frontispiece to the French translation of Johannes Tinctoris, *Tractatus contra sectum Valdensium*. The Waldensians were sometimes confounded with the witches, and writers such as Tinctoris used the term *Valdensis* or *vaudois* to designate a witch. Here the witches are shown adoring their master, who has appeared to them in the form of a goat.

75

Carlo Ginzburg recently investigated the only reliable evidence for the existence of a fertility cult in the period of the craze.[26] In Friuli, northern Italy, the *benandanti* were members of a group that practised rites to insure the fertility of the fields and a good harvest. But the inquisitors associated these rites with the Canon Episcopi and the nocturnal gatherings to worship Diana/Holda, and thus translated the meetings of the *benandanti* into diabolical sabbats.

From the beginning of the fourteenth century onwards the concept of witchcraft underwent little further development, remaining almost static for the next three hundred years. Some geographical variations persisted. In England, for example, as we have seen, the *maleficia* – evil sorceries – of the witches were emphasized much more than the linkage of witchcraft with heresy (of which there was relatively little in England). In Scotland, the term coven, a variant of convent, from Latin *conventus*, 'assembly', was introduced about 1500 as a name for the witches' meeting and then, by extension, as a name for the local group of practising witches. The term was seldom used until the modern witchcraft revival. In Spain, the relatively scrupulous fairness of the Spanish inquisition generally limited the manifestations of witchcraft in that country to simple sorcery. Diabolical witchcraft developed primarily in France, Germany, Switzerland, the Low Countries, and northern Italy – areas where heresy had been strong – and then spread into Scandinavia in the sixteenth and seventeenth centuries.

The growth of the witch-craze

The early fourteenth century produced the first vicious use of witch accusations for political purposes. Often in this early stage of the craze the accused were clergymen or other learned people who were capable of reading and writing magic. (By the end of the fourteenth century, accusations had spread more widely to ordinary people.) Pope Boniface VIII (d. 1303) was tried posthumously by his enemies for apostasy, murder, and sodomy. He allegedly entered into a pact with the Devil for the purpose of encompassing the ruin of the Christian people. Popes had been deposed before and accused of crimes, but the charge of demonolatry was new. Philip IV of France accused Bishop Guichard of Troyes of doing homage to the Devil. Under Edward I of England (1272–1307) accusations of *maleficia* were brought against Walter, bishop of Lichfield and Coventry. In 1317–19, Pope John XXII, obsessed with fear of witchcraft, accused a doctor, a barber, and a clergyman of plotting against his life through magic. Pope John went on to issue the bull *Super illius specula*, specifically authorizing the inquisition to proceed against all sorcerers, since they adored demons and had made 'a pact with hell'. The inquisitor Bernard Gui affirmed that witchcraft implied pact, pact implied heresy, and since the inquisition had the duty to proceed against heretics it also had the duty to proceed against witches. But politicians, not inquisitors, engineered the infamous trial of the Templars in 1305–14.

Originally the Order of the Temple had been founded to liberate the Holy Land from the Muslims, but the Templars had become rich and corrupt and now presented a tempting target to rulers whose governmental costs were

The burning of Jacques de Molay and a companion, 19 March 1313. De Molay, the Grand Master of the Templars, and other Templars were executed by Philip the Fair of France on charges resembling witchcraft.

rapidly rising. Pope Clement V, King Philip IV of France, and King Edward II of England succeeded in having the Templars condemned as heretics, claiming that they invoked the Devil, rendered him homage, veneration, and service, and made a pact with him. The fame and eminence of the case spread the belief that an organized religion rejecting Christ and worshipping Satan existed.

The middle years of the fourteenth century saw a lull in the craze.* Then, towards the end of the century, the number of accusations increased. Many secular courts adopted inquisitorial procedures, doing away with judicial penalties for accusers failing to prove their cases. Secular, episcopal, and inquisitorial courts shared the burden, and the profit, of the witch prosecutions down through the fifteenth century. In 1398 the University of Paris declared the working of *maleficia* a heresy if it was accomplished through pact with the Devil. The pact might be explicit or implicit. No document needed to be signed or official promise given: the mere act of summoning demons constituted an implied pact and rendered the accused subject to prosecution for heresy. In such an atmosphere witch trials began to take on a standard form. Inquisitors' manuals listed the questions that were to be put to the accused, and torture or fear of torture readily elicited confessions such as those of 1387–8 in Lombardy. A small group was arrested for heresy. In the

*The evidence for substantial witch trials at Toulouse and Carcassonne in the period 1330–50 has been proven a forgery.

77

course of the interrogation they were tortured and compelled to implicate most of the town in the crime. Though their basic doctrines seem to have been a mixture of Waldensianism and Catharism, they confessed that both men and women in 'synagogue' once or twice a month formally renounced the Catholic faith and adored Satan as their God. Satan, they claimed, would one day defeat Christ. They feasted and drank loathsome potions; then, with lights extinguished, they fell to an orgy where each seized the one next him. These clichés were derived from the inquisitorial model, and each trial reinforced the model.

As belief and confessions reinforced one another, the number of trials increased radically, especially in France, Germany, and the Alps. In a book about the trials Richard Kieckhefer argues that the prime responsibility falls on the intellectuals.[27] Accusations commonly began, he says, with charges of simple sorcery. The courts, whether secular, ecclesiastical, or inquisitorial, then presented the accused with a list of the crimes the courts expected, and the original charge of sorcery was transformed into witchcraft.

The standardization of witch accusations produced a dramatic change in the powers assigned to the Devil. Hitherto, the witch making a pact with Satan enjoyed almost a contractual equality with the dark lord; further, she was frequently rescued from the effects of her folly by the intervention of the Virgin or another saint. Now, the Devil's power over her once she had made the pact was complete, and her soul was damned. Her only hope of salvation was to be arrested and to recant before her execution. By such reasoning the torment and killing of witches was for their own good as well as that of God and of society.

Joan of Arc and Gilles de Rais both frequently appear in histories of witchcraft, but neither is relevant. Witch charges were very much in the background in both trials. Joan was condemned – for political reasons of course – on charges of heresy, not of witchcraft. Gilles was a sexual pervert and murderer whose alleged activities bear no resemblance to those alleged against the witches.

The trial of an old man in southern France in 1438 is typical of the period. Pierre Vallin was charged with witchcraft and seized by the inquisition. Allowed no defence, he was repeatedly tortured. The record of the trial states that he made his confession 'voluntarily', which simply means that he was tortured, removed from the place of torture, and then given the choice of confessing voluntarily or of being returned for more torture. Pierre confessed to invoking Beelzebub, to whom he used habitually to kneel and pay tribute. He had served the Devil for sixty-three years, during which time he had denied God, trampled and spat on the cross, and sacrificed his own baby daughter. He went regularly to the 'synagogue', where he copulated with Beelzebub, who had taken the form of a girl – only this is unusual – and where he and the other witches ate the flesh of innocent children. The judges condemned him as a heretic, idolater, apostate, and invoker of demons. All his worldly possessions were confiscated and, after the expenses of the trial were deducted, a third of what remained was reserved for the archbishop and the inquisition. But that was not enough. Pierre was required to name his accomplices. He was tortured again and again for a week, until he had named a number of people. His ultimate fate and theirs is not known, but it is almost certain that they were burned to death. The inquisitors' repeated efforts to persuade Pierre to name not only poor men but 'priests, clergymen, nobles and rich men' indicate that thoughts of confiscation were not absent from their minds.

Tens of thousands of such trials continued throughout Europe generation after generation, while Leonardo painted, Palestrina composed, and Shakespeare wrote. The witches in *Macbeth* may be difficult to take seriously today, but *Macbeth* was written in the reign of James I, who hanged more witches than any other English monarch.

The craze, far from declining at the end of the fifteenth century, took on new strength. In large part this was owing to the efforts of the German inquisitor Heinrich Institoris. Institoris, born near Strasbourg about 1430, entered the Dominican Order. A clever politician, he acquired influential friends in Rome and was appointed inquisitor in southern Germany in 1474. At first he investigated heresy but in 1476 began to devote himself almost exclusively to witchcraft. Helped at first by his Dominican colleague Jakob Sprenger, who later repented and condemned him, Institoris compiled a record of great severity and corruption. He was condemned by his own Order in 1490 for embezzlement and other crimes, but he was still active as a witch-hunter at the turn of the century. Through his influence at the papal court, he persuaded Innocent VIII to issue the bull *Summis Desiderantes Affectibus*, 'Wishing with the greatest concern' (1484), which confirmed full papal support for the work of the inquisition against witches.

In 1486, Institoris published the *Malleus Maleficarum*, 'the Hammer against the Witches', with the pope's approval and with the bull of 1484 as preface. The *Malleus* was reprinted in fourteen editions by 1520. Well-organized, impassioned, and enjoying papal approval, the *Malleus* became one of the most influential of all early printed books. Its influence overwhelmed the moderate tradition within the Catholic Church. The *Malleus* declared that the four essential points of witchcraft were: renunciation of the Catholic faith, devotion of body and soul to the service of evil, offering up unbaptized children to the Devil, and engaging in orgies that included intercourse with the Devil. In addition, witches typically shifted their shapes, flew through the air, abused the Christian sacraments, and confected magical ointments. The great majority of witches were women, and the reason for this is, Institoris declared, that women are more stupid, fickle, lighter-headed, weaker, and more carnal than men. All witches, men and women, must be accused, arrested, convicted, and executed.

With the *Malleus*, witchcraft theory caught up with and surpassed the practice of the courts. In his description of the witch trials in Lorraine, Etienne Delcambre argues that most judges were honest, sincere, and idealistic men who believed that they were performing a necessary service for society, God, and even the accused, whose soul they hoped to save by extracting confession.[28] If a person were innocent of the accusations, they believed that God would intervene to save him from torment. Delcambre suggests that often the accused may have shared this belief, for in Lorraine only 10 per cent persisted in denying their guilt to the moment of death, the

Swimming a witch. One of the common tests of witchcraft was to throw the witch into deep water. If the water, God's creature, rejected her and she floated, she was guilty. If she sank, she was innocent. Two men hold her with ropes so as to draw her up again if she sinks.

rest confessing in the hope of obtaining a gentler execution or of sparing their families further persecution. Some of the accused even took the opportunity to bring personal enemies down with them in death. One defendant in the region of Bar accused all the officers of the court from the judges down to the court clerk of being witches. On the whole, the use of torture is sufficient explanation for most of the confessions.

Some torments were designed to test the guilt or innocence of the witch, such as 'swimming'. A survival of the ancient ordeal by water, 'swimming the witch' involved tying the accused hand and foot and throwing her into deep water. If she sank, it was a sign that God's creature water accepted her, and she was deemed innocent and hauled ashore. If she floated, the water rejected her, and she was judged guilty. Another test was weighing. The witch was placed on one side of the scale and the Bible on the other. If the witch weighed lighter than the Bible, she was guilty. Another was pricking. Witches were thought to have insensitive spots on their bodies where the Devil had marked them. Sometimes these Devil's marks were visible as a scar or mole, but sometimes they were invisible and could be detected only by pricking the accused all over with a sharp instrument until such an area of

insensitivity were found. Another was the search for the witch's mark. The witch's mark, quite distinct from the Devil's mark, was any unusual protuberance on the body that could conceivably be considered a supernumerary teat that the demons might suck in the form of familiars. Witches were stripped and searched minutely for any such sign of their traffic with evil.

Other tortures were devised to elicit confessions and the implication of accomplices. The infamous witch-house of Bamberg contained thumb-screws, leg vices, whipping stocks furnished with iron spikes, scalding lime baths, prayer stools furnished with sharp pegs, racks, the strappado and other devices. In the strappado, the prisoner's

In the strappado, the prisoner's 'arms were tied behind his back with a rope attached to a pulley, and he was then hoisted in the air'.

arms were tied behind his back with a rope attached to a pulley, and he was then hoisted in the air. Frequently, weights were attached to his feet to pull his shoulders from their sockets without leaving visible marks of rough treatment. Sometimes toescrews and thumbscrews were applied while the victim was suspended.[29]

The tortured were confronted by standard lists of questions and in their agony usually confessed to most of what was put to them. Each confession convinced the authorities of the validity of the lists and reinforced their use at the next trial. The list prepared for the judges at Colmar in Alsace is typical:

How long have you been a witch? Why did you become a witch? How did you become a witch, and what happened on the occasion? [What demon did you choose to be your lover?] What was his name? What was the name of your master among the evil demons? What was the oath you were forced to render him? How did you make this oath, and what were its conditions? . . . Where did you consummate your union with your incubus? What demons and what other humans participated [at the sabbat]? . . . How was the sabbat banquet arranged? . . . What devil's mark did your incubus make on your body? What injury have you done to such and such a person, and how did you do it? . . . Who are the children on whom you have cast a spell? . . . Who are your accomplices in evil? . . . What is the ointment with which you rub your broomstick made of? How are you able to fly through the air?[30]

The question was not whether you had done it, but when and how you had done it.

The Protestant Reformation of the sixteenth century aimed at eradicating the accretions of doctrine in the Middle Ages and insisted upon a return to the apostolic age. But one accretion of doctrine they did not choose to jettison was belief in witchcraft. The Protestants pursued witches with comparable cruelty and in comparable numbers to the Catholics. Luther argued with his typical violence that all witches should be burned as heretics for having made a pact with the Devil, even if there was no evidence that they had done anyone any overt harm. The witches, he said, were an important battalion in the vast legion of enemies that the Devil was assembling against the true Church. Calvin, whose doctrines emphasized the omnipotence of God, found less room for witchcraft in his theology than Lutherans or Catholics, but he accepted the reality of witchcraft and its danger to Christian society. Persecutions in Calvinist territories were (except at Geneva itself) comparable to those in other regions.

In Germany the Protestants were more severe in the sixteenth century and the Catholics in the seventeenth. In France, the Catholics were worse, but in countries won to the Protestant cause, such as England, Scotland, and Scandinavia, the persecutions were nearly as bad. In some Catholic countries, such as Spain and Portugal, very few witch trials occurred. Variations in time and region were great, but in general the Protestants do not seem to have taken advantage of the fact that they were not bound by the views of the *Malleus* and of the bull of Innocent VIII. These documents were based upon a long tradition of witch beliefs that the Protestants accepted as fully as did the Catholics.

Prosecution of witches by Christians of all persuasions increased enormously in the sixteenth century, as the religious conflicts, popular movements, and wars engendered by the Reformation exacerbated the social tensions that produced witchcraft. The 'Caroline Code' or *Constitutio Criminalis Carolina*, the basic law code of the Holy Roman Empire issued in 1532, imposed heavy penalties on witchcraft. Witch fears were also fuelled by the increasing number of tracts and books on popular theology issued for an increasingly literate population, books that emphasized the power of the Devil and portrayed him as responsible for most human sins and vices.

The height of the witch-craze occurred between 1560 and 1660. Increasing tensions between Protestant and Catholic, worsening into war, were the most important cause. The craze was most severe in areas where religious strife was linked with strong social antagonisms, where misfortunes such as storms, plagues, and famines heightened social tensions, and wherever, as in France, a long tradition of heresy trials had laid the basis for judicial repression of witchcraft. Both ecclesiastical and secular prosecution of witchcraft increased greatly in scope and severity during these years, particularly in the Catholic areas of Europe. After 1580, the more thorough Jesuits replaced the Dominicans as the chief Catholic witch-hunters, and the Catholic Rudolf II (1576–1612) presided over a long and cruel persecution in Austria. Geographical variations in the trials continued to occur. William Monter has shown that witch panics were not so severe in the Jura Mountains as in southern Germany and that in the Jura many arrested suspects were not convicted. In the Jura, Monter explains, torture was imposed only within the precise limits of the Caroline code of 1532, little attention was paid to the accusations and confessions of children, and specific *maleficia* had to be charged openly and publicly against a suspect before he could be arrested.[31] Such legal limitations could contain the mania; in areas where they were ignored, anyone and everyone could be accused.

Rossell Hope Robbins has charged that the chief motive behind the prosecutions was the desire to appropriate the property of the condemned. If this were so, we would expect to find a relatively high percentage of rich and powerful people condemned and a large over-all number of decrees of confiscation. In fact we find neither. The number of confiscations was relatively small, and a disproportionately great number of people convicted were of small means. It was generally only in areas where the craze was completely out of hand that people of substantial means were convicted. One of the exceptions was Dietrich Flade, burned at Trier for witchcraft in 1589.

Flade was a secular judge at Trier, a man of prominent family and connections who became rector of the University of Trier. For a while he was himself in charge of the prosecution of witches. In that capacity he was judicious and restrained, demanding careful presentation of evidence. His moderation was fiercely opposed by the suffragan bishop Peter Binsfeld and the governor, Johann Zandt, who had had experience as a witch-hunter in the countryside around Trier. The efforts of Binsfeld and Zandt to obtain fiercer prosecution of witches gathered popular support after 1580 when bad climatic conditions, plagues of mice and locusts, and ravaging freebooters of both religious persuasions rendered people fearful and anxious. Times were bad: the witches must be responsible. Flade's continued efforts to keep the mania under control led his enemies to devise a plan to remove him. They caused a boy to accuse Flade of plotting to poison the archbishop; they persuaded an old woman who was about to be executed to name Flade as a witch in order to obtain the mercy of strangulation before burning; other accusations followed, until on 15 April 1588 a woman swore that she had seen Flade at a sabbat, that he had caused the destruction of crops by hail, slugs, and snails, and that he had persuaded the other witches present to eat a child's heart. Flade was arrested and tortured. His pain was intense, and he finally confessed that he had attended sabbats, had intercourse with the Devil, and magically formed mud into living slugs to destroy the crops. Flade was strangled and burnt, but not before he had been forced under torture to name accomplices, thus widening the circle of accusations, assuring Binsfeld and Zandt of more victims, and providing the peasants more scapegoats for their troubles.

Simple people were much more frequently accused than prominent men such as Flade. In 1587 Walpurga Hausmannin, a midwife, was tried and burnt at Dillingen. Arrested and tortured, she admitted to having intercourse with the Devil and making pact with him, riding out at night on a pitchfork, trampling on the consecrated host, keeping a familiar named Federlin as a lover, manufacturing hailstorms, and committing a long list of *maleficia* relating to her duties as midwife. She rubbed Anna Hämännin during childbirth with a salve that caused both mother and child to die. She crushed the brain of Dorothea Wachter's baby while delivering it. She poisoned the child of Anna Kromt. She rubbed a salve on the son of the Chancellor, giving the boy a hobby horse to ride until he lost his senses and died. She sucked the blood out of one of the twin children of the publican Kuntz. Forty-three of these charges of *maleficia* were combined with the accusations of demon-worship.[32] The process is simple. A number of children die. The midwife is a lonely and unpopular widow. Blame for the deaths is fixed on her and expressed in supernatural terms. She must therefore be a witch. But it is well known that all witches fly out at night, make pacts with the Devil, and practise other kinds of demonolatry. Questions about all this are put to her under torture, and in her agony and fear she confesses. The confession again reinforces the accepted image of the witch. Misfortunes are interpreted as evil deeds, evil deeds are seen as sorcery, sorcery is perceived as witchcraft, and another human being is tortured and killed.

Some contemporaries recognized the injustice. In 1563, Johann Weyer wrote a treatise *On Magic*, which argued that witches are really harmless old women suffering from mental disorders and that most alleged cases of witchcraft are really susceptible of natural explanations. But Jean Bodin and other intellectual leaders hastened to refute this voice of moderation, accusing Weyer himself of being a witch, and arguing that the similarity of the confessions proved the fact that the sabbat was always and everywhere identical. A little later, in 1602, Henri Boguet wrote in his *Discours des sorciers* that he wished that all witches should be 'united in one single body, so that they might all be burned at once in a single fire.' This mania, this eagerness to torture and kill human beings, persisted for centuries. Perhaps we put the wrong question when we ask how this could be. The past half-century has witnessed the Holocaust, the Gulag Archipelago, the Cambodian genocide, and secret tortures and executions beyond number. The real question is why periods of relative sanity, such as those from 700 to 1000 and from 1700 to 1900, occur.

For the seventeenth century was as bloody as the sixteenth. A century of religious strife culminated in the Thirty Years War of 1618–48 that ravaged

VINCE
TE
IPSUM

Joannes Wierus

Johann Wier or Weyer. Weyer was the author of a courageous treatise against indiscriminate prosecution of witches. For his trouble, he was himself accused of being a witch.

Germany and involved most of Europe. In such a time the persecutions increased, notably at Cologne in 1625–36 and in Bamberg, where from 1623 to 1633 Bishop Johann Georg II burnt at least 600 witches, trying them in the notorious 'witch-house', mentioned above, where he had constructed a torture chamber whose walls were adorned by biblical texts. It was at Bamberg that one of the most infamous prosecutions occurred, that of Johannes Junius.

Junius was examined on 28 June 1628. Maintaining his innocence, he demanded to be confronted with a single human being who had seen him at a sabbat. One Doctor Georg Haan, probably hoping to buy mercy for himself by accusing others, was brought in and swore on his own life that he had seen Junius a year and a half earlier at a sabbat. Next a servant woman swore that she had seen him at a sabbat where the Eucharist was desecrated. Junius denied both accusations, but he was warned that other accomplices had confessed against him and that he had best admit his crimes. On 30 June he was examined again, though the threatened witnesses did not appear, and he again refused to confess. He was then tortured, first with thumbscrews and then with legscrews. He was stripped and examined, and a bluish mark was found on his right side. This Devil's mark was pricked. He was then put to the strappado. On 5 July, 'without torture, but with urgent persuasions' – i.e., threat of torture – Junius at last confessed to worshipping the Devil, attending the sabbats, performing *maleficia*, and other clichés of witchcraft.

What makes Junius unusually interesting is that he was able to bribe the jailer before his execution to smuggle out a letter. It is dated 24 July 1628 and is addressed to his daughter:

Many hundred thousand good-nights, dearly beloved daughter Veronica. Innocent have I come into prison, innocent have I been tortured, innocent must I die. For whoever comes into the witch prison must . . . be tortured until he invents something out of his head. . . . When I was the first time put to the torture, Dr Braun, Dr Kötzendörffer, and two strange doctors were there. Then Dr Braun asks me, 'Kinsman, how come you here?' I answer, 'Through falsehood, though misfortune.' 'Hear, you,' he retorts, 'you are a witch; will you confess it voluntarily? If not, we'll bring in witnesses and the executioner for you.' I said, 'I am no witch, I have a pure conscience in the matter; if there are a thousand witnesses, I am not anxious.' [The witnesses were brought forward.] And then came also – God in highest heaven have mercy – the executioner, and put the thumb-screws on me, both hands bound together, so that the blood ran out at the nails and everywhere, so that for four weeks I could not use my hands, as you can see from the writing. . . . Thereafter they first stripped me, bound my hands behind me, and drew me up in the [strappado]. Then I thought heaven and earth were at an end; eight times did they draw me up and let me fall again, so that I suffered terrible agony. . . . And so I made my confession . . ., but it was all a lie. Now follows, dear child, what I confessed in order to escape the great anguish and bitter torture, which it was impossible for me longer to bear. [He reported his confession.] Then I had to tell what people I had seen [at the sabbat]. I said that I had not recognized them. 'You old rascal, I must set the executioner at you. Say – was not the Chancellor there?' So I said yes. 'Who besides?' I had not recognized anybody. So he said: 'Take one street after another; begin at the market, go out on one street and back on the next.' I had to name several persons there. Then came the long street. I knew nobody. Had to name eight persons there. . . . And thus

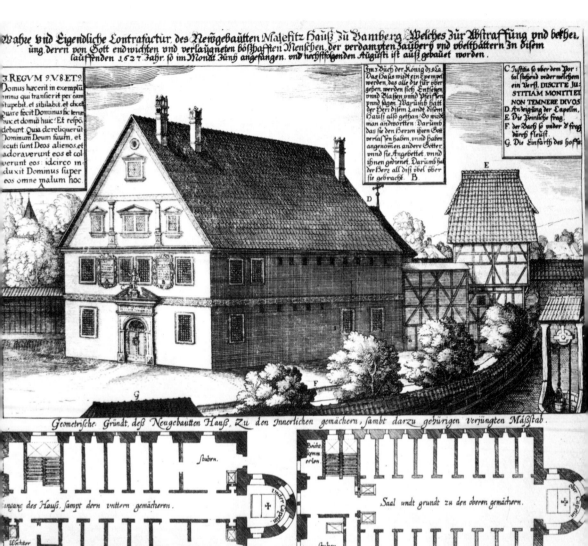

The witch-house at Bamberg.
Constructed by Bishop
Johann Georg II, it contained
prison cells and notorious
torture chambers.

continually they asked me on all the streets, though I could not and would not say more. So they gave me to the executioner, told him to strip me, shave me all over, and put me to the torture. . . . Then I had to tell what crimes I had committed. I said nothing. . . . 'Draw the rascal up!' So I said that I was to kill my children, but I had killed a horse instead. It did not help. I had also taken a sacred wafer, and had desecrated it. When I had said this, they left me in peace. . . . Dear child, keep this letter secret . . . else I shall be tortured most piteously and the jailers will be beheaded. . . . Good night, for your father Johannes Junius will never see you more.[33]

Witchcraft hysteria produced a number of bizarre by-products in the early seventeenth century, among them cases of diabolism in convents, notably at

87

EFFIGIE DE LA CONDEMNATION DE MORT
& execution d'Vrbain Grandier, Curé de l'Eglise S. Pierre du Marché de Loudun, atteint
& conuaincu de Magie, fortileges & malefic s, lequel a cfté bruflé vif en ladite ville.

Father Urbain Grandier, confessor at the Ursuline convent of Loudun, dies at the stake in 1630. In the background can be seen the crazed nuns whose feigned fits and acts of indecency led to Grandier's conviction on a charge of witchcraft.

Aix-en-Provence in 1611, Loudun in 1630, and Louviers in 1647. Not typical of witchcraft, these cases nonetheless illustrate the obsession of society with witchcraft and diabolism, and how under certain conditions frightened and suggestible people readily believed themselves to be in communion with Satan.

The story of the nuns of Loudun, made infamous by the novel of Aldous Huxley and the film of Ken Russell, requires little embroidery. It began as a plot by the enemies of Father Urbain Grandier, confessor at the Ursuline convent of Loudun. The mother superior and several of the nuns pretended to be possessed and accused Father Grandier of bewitching them. They feigned convulsions, rolled and gibbered on the ground, and accused Grandier of numerous indecencies. Grandier was no exemplary priest, but the evidence that he was a witch was deliberately and cleverly faked, including a silly alleged pact written right to left in Latin and signed by Satan, Beelzebub, Lucifer, Leviathan, and other evil spirits, one of whom marked his name with a drawing of a pitchfork. In spite of such ridiculous subterfuges, and despite the fact that many of the nuns who had accused the priest publicly recanted, Grandier's enemies were not to be deterred. He was tortured lengthily and denied even the small grace of strangulation before being placed in the flames.

But now events took an odd turn. The original plot having succeeded, no reasons remained for the nuns to feign possession. Yet their symptoms only grew worse. One nun

fell to the ground, blaspheming, in convulsions, lifting up her petticoats and chemise, displaying her privy parts without any shame, and uttering filthy words. Her gestures became so indecent that the audience averted its eyes. She cried out again and again, abusing herself with her hands, 'Come on, then, f— me!' [At other times the nuns] struck their chests and backs with their heads, as if they had their necks broken, and with inconceivable rapidity. . . . Their faces became so frightful one could not bear to look at them; their eyes remained open without winking. Their tongues issued suddenly from their mouths, horribly swollen, black, hard, and covered with pimples. . . . They threw themselves back till their heads touched their feet, and walked in this position with wonderful rapidity, and for a long time. They uttered cries so horrible and so loud that nothing like it was ever heard before. They made use of expressions so indecent as to shame the most debauched of men. . . .[34]

From pretending to be possessed, the nuns had in fact come to believe themselves possessed. Delusion had bred psychosis. Such events indicate the degree to which the social mania of witchcraft produced insanity in individuals.

But the fever was already past its peak. In 1687 Louis XIV issued an edict against *sorcellerie*. It was refreshingly moderate; condemning sorcery, it ignored black cats, sex-crazed nuns, and other lurid fantasies of the witch-mania. The worst was over. After 1700, the number of witches accused, tried and condemned fell off rapidly. The decline of the witch-craze is as interesting as its rise, but before we lay it to rest we will want to look at its course in Britain and the American colonies.

5 *Witchcraft in Britain and America*

WITCHCRAFT IN THE BRITISH ISLES

Witchcraft in the British Isles differed substantially from continental witchcraft. On the continent, heresy, law, theology, and inquisition transformed the old traditions of sorcery into a cult of Satan. But in England there was no inquisition, no Roman law, and only a weak tradition of heresy. The most important medieval dissent in England, that of the Lollards, was a moderate heresy with few continental connections, and it was never associated with witchcraft. English witchcraft remained closer to sorcery, though with greatly increased emphasis upon the negative powers of the witch to hex and curse. Notorious political cases such as that of the Duchess of Gloucester, accused in 1441 of plotting to kill Henry VI by witchcraft, abetted the rise of the delusion, but during the Middle Ages the British Isles were almost free of the concept of witchcraft as devil-worship.

The one important medieval exception proving the rule is unusual in almost every respect. This is the case of Dame Alice Kyteler. Dame Alice lived in Kilkenny in Ireland, and the case shows signs of Irish folk-elements as well as the more usual aspects of witchcraft and sorcery. Alice was a wealthy woman who had had four husbands and who infuriated her elder children by bequeathing all her property to her youngest child. In 1324, the elder children accused their mother and her companions before the bishop, who condemned her as a heretic and magician. The introduction of the charge of heresy is incongruous in fourteenth-century Ireland, and the catalogue of charges brought against Dame Alice is a strange mélange of English, continental, and Irish ideas. The most probable explanation is that for venal and political motives the bishop, Richard Ledrede, who had lived in London and knew something about the continental tradition, put together a hodgepodge of charges in order to gratify Alice's sons.

According to the account of the trial, Dame Alice had renounced Christ and the Church in order to obtain magical powers. She had sacrificed animals to demons, notably to her familiar, a minor demon by the name of Robert or Robin Artisson. Robin, one of the first named familiars in witchcraft, was probably a version of an Irish folk spirit to whom the attributes of continental demons were attached by Bishop Ledrede. Robin appeared as a cat, a shaggy dog, or a black man; as a black man he was accompanied by two taller comrades, one of whom bore an iron rod in his hands. These demons taught Lady Alice the arts of witchcraft, and under their instruction she learned to make loathsome ointments and other concoctions. She gave everything she possessed to the demons (the not too

Opposite: a witch and her familiars, from *A Discourse of Witchcraft*, 1621. A familiar is a demon who accompanies and serves the witch. Often they took the shape of animals, especially black cats or dogs.

Witchcraft ye practice of deluded minds,
Where grace is wanting soon admission finds.
With golden promisses of life & wealth,
The Tempter takes unwary souls by stealth.
In this his seeming clemency appears,
That he will give them back a lease for years.
But ye expir'd, how dismall is their end!
And case, when he a Feind shall for them send.
Tis death to think of mending when too late,
And glories given for so vile a rate.
As power to hurt another, & to sin
With greater freedom, from controll within.
That Laws Divine, & humane, should not be
The least restraint, to their impiety.
That reason should be set aside, & death
Become their choice, when they resigne their breath
That piety should be of no esteem,
Nor Faith in him, that only can redeem.
All their conceited pleasures come to this,
When yelling they discend ye grand Abyss.

subtle hand of Alice's elder sons is visible in this charge), and they straightway returned it for her use during her lifetime. Robin was Alice's demon lover, and at night the lady would gather her associates by candlelight. Blowing out the candles and calling out 'Fi fi fi, amen', they would fall to a sexual orgy. Alice and her friends were a group of twelve, so that with Robin as their master they mocked the number of Christ and his apostles. The concept and name of coven were as yet two hundred years in the future, but the notion that a heresiarch would take twelve followers in imitation of Christ and the apostles was longstanding in the history of continental heresy. Dame Alice escaped with a fine, but at least one of her less influential associates was burnt.

The Kyteler case had little if any influence on subsequent trials, and the wide gap separating English from continental witchcraft continued well into the sixteenth century. Though the *Malleus Maleficarum* enjoyed fourteen editions by 1520, it had no English translation until modern times. As late as the 1560s, Essex witches differed markedly from their continental colleagues: they did not fly, meet for orgies, dance and feast, or practise sexual perversions. Most significantly, they did not sign a pact with the Devil or worship him. Rather, English witches, like African sorcerers, caused disease and fits, harmed livestock, hurt infants and small children, and kept familiars. Familiars were found on the continent, especially in Germany, but they were commonest in England, where they had curious names such as Vinegar Tom, Pyewacket, Tibb, Sack and Sugar, or Grizel Greediguts. Is it possible that the English and German predilection for familiars stemmed from their fondness for pets? But these beings were in their origins the little people of folklore, transformed by Christian theology into demons and hence acquiring sinister attributes: they had intercourse with the witches, or sucked the blood of their mistresses through 'witches' teats'. The search for the witches' teat, or supernumerary protuberance, was one of the most appalling aspects of prosecution for witchcraft in England. In Scotland, pricking was more in favour. Concern about witchcraft was still moderate in England through the reign of Elizabeth I. John Dee (1527–1608), a magician having considerable influence at court, had a large library on all aspects of magic, including continental witchcraft, but continental ideas were still far from English practice.

The first statute against witchcraft in England was passed by Parliament in 1542, towards the end of the reign of Henry VIII, and it was soon revoked in 1547. A new statute was issued under Elizabeth I in 1563, ordering the death penalty for witches, enchanters, and sorcerers. These individuals were to be prosecuted under civil, not ecclesiastical law, and for this reason witches in England were always hanged rather than burnt as on the continent.

The first major trial under the statute of 1563 was at Chelmsford in Essex in 1566, a trial setting an unhappy precedent for later cases. Elizabeth Francis, Agnes Waterhouse, and Agnes' daughter Joan were charged with witchcraft. Elizabeth had supposedly bewitched a child and committed other evil deeds or *maleficia*. Such were the charges originally brought, but a confession she allegedly made expanded the scope of her crimes considerably. According to the confession, she had learned witchcraft from her

grandmother when she was twelve years old. The grandmother taught her to renounce God and gave her a white spotted cat named Sathan, who was in fact the Devil in animal form. Elizabeth was to nourish it with her own blood as well as with more traditional bread and milk. Elizabeth learned to speak with the cat, who promised her (in a hollow voice) that she would have riches. Sathan brought her livestock and promised her one Andrew Byles as a husband; when Byles refused marriage after enjoying her favours,

John Dee, court magician to Elizabeth I. Not himself con-nected with witchcraft, his prominence indicates the prevalence of a world view in which witchcraft was an accepted phenomenon.

93

Sathan caused his death and taught her how to abort the child that she was carrying. She later married and had a daughter, but the infant annoyed her, and she caused Sathan to murder it. Finally, after enjoying the cat's help for sixteen years, she gave it to Agnes Waterhouse in exchange for a cake. Agnes, wishing to divert to other purposes the wool that lined the cat's box, changed his Satanic Majesty into a toad; with its help Agnes effected a number of *maleficia*, drowning cows, killing geese, and spoiling butter. Both Elizabeth and Agnes gave Sathan blood which they produced by pricking their bodies; the evidence was found in the shape of blemishes on the bodies of the accused. Agnes was hanged in 1566 (her daughter Joan was found not guilty); Elizabeth received a lighter sentence but was hanged after a second conviction thirteen years later. The Chelmsford trial was typical of English witchcraft in many ways: the absurdity of the charges, the emphasis upon the familiar, and the lack of the classic, continental insistence upon pact, orgy, and homage to the Devil.

At the Essex assizes of 1579 several women were arraigned for witchcraft. Ellen Smythe was one of them. Her daughter had had a quarrel with a child named Susan Webbe. Encountering Susan, Ellen gave the child a blow on the head, so that two days later she died. Directly after her death, Susan's mother saw 'a thing like a black dog go out of her door'. Ellen was hanged. Margery Stanton used magic to kill chickens, causing a woman to swell up as if pregnant, and cattle to give blood instead of milk. She was released for lack of evidence against her. Joan or Jane Prentice, charged at the assize of 1589, first encountered the Devil while sitting in her chamber. He came to her in the form of a 'dunnish coloured ferret' and said, 'Jane Prentice, give me thy soul.' She replied: 'In the name of God, what art thou?' And the ferret returned: 'I am Satan; fear me not.' Jane Prentice was also hanged.[35]

This was fertile soil for the sowing of continental ideas. These eventually made their way to England by way of Scotland, whose King James VI was a learned proponent of the witch-craze. James was convinced of the reality of witchcraft by the trial of the North Berwick witches in 1590–92. A young girl named Gilly Duncan had the reputation of being able to aid and cure the sick. Her employer, convinced that she must have diabolical powers, took it upon himself to torture her until she confessed that she had received help from the Devil. Justified by her confession, he turned her over for prosecution, and under threat of further torture Gilly accused a large number of men and women in and around Edinburgh. One of these, Agnes Sampson, an elderly woman of good education and reputation, was examined by the king himself. Since she refused to confess, she was stripped, shaved, and searched until the devil's mark was found.

She was fastened to the wall of her cell by a witch's bridle, an iron instrument with four sharp prongs forced into the mouth, so that two prongs pressed against the tongue, and the two others against the cheeks. She was kept without sleep.[36]

Not surprisingly, Agnes eventually confessed. A large company of men and women had sailed in sieves to North Berwick on Hallowe'en, she said. They danced, entered a church illuminated by black candles, and did homage to the Devil in the form of a man, whose buttocks they kissed. The witches

Opposite: execution of the Chelmsford witches, 1589. Essex was the county of England most affected by the witch-craze. Here three victims are shown hanged. Joan Prentice, one of the victims, is also shown with her familiars, two of whom are named 'Jack' and 'Jill'.

¶ The Apprehension and confession
of three notorious Witches.

Arreigned and by Iustice condemned and
executed at *Chelmes-forde*, in the Countye of
Essex, *the 5. day of Iulye, last past.*
1 5 8 9.

¶ With the manner of their diuelish practices and keeping of their
spirits, whose fourmes are heerein truelye
proportioned.

James I of England and VI of Scotland. King James, a devout monarch who authorized a new translation of the Bible, also wrote a credulous book on witchcraft entitled *Daemonologie*, which introduced continental witch ideas into England.

plotted to raise a storm to sink the king's ship as he sailed to Denmark; if this failed, Agnes planned to work magic against the king with toad's blood. The evidence given by Agnes and the other accused brought many of them to the stake, a punishment approved under Scottish law. This trial had great influence because of James' attention to it, and it set the pattern for many seventeenth-century trials in both Scotland and England.

The bulk of learned opinion in England remained moderate throughout the sixteenth century. Reginald Scot's *Discoverie of Witchcraft* (1584) offered a distinctively Protestant argument against belief in witchcraft. Protestants affirmed that the age of miracles had ended with the death of the last apostle. Since God no longer worked marvels himself, Scot argued, he clearly would no longer permit the Devil to do so. But the age of relative tolerance was brought to an end by the succession of James VI to the English throne in 1603 as James I. James, who had developed a deep terror of witches as a result of the North Berwick incident, was enough of a scholar to be familiar with the continental books and arguments. In 1597 he had published his *Daemonologie*, a direct attack upon Scot and upon the German sceptic Weyer. A good Calvinist, James based his chief argument for the existence of witches upon predestination. Man was made in God's image, but he had lost that image through original sin. God restored the image to the elect through grace, but all the rest of mankind are 'given over in the handes of the Devill that enemie, to beare his Image', and thus take pleasure in the 'grossest impietie'. The grossest impiety was the worship of God's greatest enemy, the Devil. Since those who were not elect were followers of the Devil, it was natural that some should openly follow their dark lord in the witch-cult. The king commanded his Christian subjects to be diligent in searching out these enemies of Christ.

When James became James I of England, he quickly introduced these continental ideas into his new kingdom. The version of the Bible that he authorized used the term 'witch' more liberally than earlier translations, and a new statute against witchcraft in 1604 established pact, devil-worship, and other continental ideas in English law. James eventually revised his own views after investigating some alleged cases of witchcraft in which fraud was obvious, but English law and beliefs had been altered.

Traditionally, Englishmen had dealt with sorcery through direct, or at least local, remedies. 'Cunning-folk', men and women comparable to the German *Hexenbanner* or African witch-doctors, offered their services for sale to those who believed that they had been hexed. The cunning-folk could provide preventative magic to ward off spells, or, once you were hexed, they could provide incantations, counter-spells, or other magical remedies. The cunning-folk could use divination, oracles, or mirrors and other reflecting surfaces to identify the witch so that you might have recourse against her. At worst, the cunning-person exposed the witch to harsh abuse and even death. Well into the nineteenth century, lynching of alleged witches occurred. The clerical and civil authorities took a dim view of the cunning-folk, as much for their usurpation of authority as for their terrorizing of the people, and it is clear that the cunning-folk and their continental counterparts have caused misery over a longer span of time than the authorities of church and state. Yet the work of the cunning-folk, and the occasional direct confrontation between supposed victim and witch were the folkways that had evolved to deal with the problem. The statutes of 1563 and 1604 erected a system of official prosecution atop this folk system.

Memories of Berwick, together with the statute of 1604, helped produce the Lancashire trial of 1612, where twenty alleged witches were tried together. The witches supposedly met secretly to feast, did bodily injury through magic, and kept a familiar demon in the form of a brown dog.

The height of the witch-craze in England occurred in the 1640s, when the Civil War produced unusual anxieties and insecurities, and particularly in Essex, a county where war tensions and a strong previous tradition of witchcraft came together. Into this opportune situation stepped an unsuccessful lawyer named Matthew Hopkins, who was to cause more people to be hanged in two years than had been hanged in the previous

CHAP. X.

How ſome Witches revelling in a Gentleman's Houſe, ſerved the Servants who
ſurpriſed them.

IT happened one time that a great number of Lancaſhire Witches were rev-
ling in a gentleman's houſe, in his ab-
ſence, and making merry with what they
found, the dogs not daring to ſtir, they
having it ſeems, power to ſtrike them
mute.—However, dnring their frolick-

The Lancashire witches. The
trial of these witches in 1612
was the first in which
continental clichés of
witchcraft were introduced.

century. Hopkins, a Puritan, was able to play on the war anxieties of the
Puritan population of Essex and convince them that a legion of witches was
active among them. At a distance it is difficult to judge Hopkins'
motivation. A man who had failed, he seems to have welcomed a chance for
fame and success no matter how achieved; he may have relished the power;
and he obtained a good deal of money for his efforts. He may even have

Frontispiece to Matthew Hopkins' *Discoverie of Witches*, 1647. The 'Witchfinder-General of England' is shown looking at two witches surrounded by their familiars.

believed in what he was doing: he relied heavily throughout his career on King James' *Daemonologie*. Whatever Hopkins' own purposes, his ministrations were well received. Making a name for himself first in 1644-5 in Chelmsford, a target for witch accusations since 1566, he then moved throughout southeastern England, appointing searchers to help him in his work.

Hopkins' methods were thorough and merciless. He stripped suspects to search for witches' marks, and used starvation, sleep deprivation, swimming, and other tests and torments. The confessions he elicited show his acceptance of the continental tradition: the witches were members of a sect worshipping the Devil; they met at night; held initiations; had sexual relations with the Devil; and sacrificed to him. Nor did Hopkins neglect English tradition: his witches kept familiars in the shape of dogs, cats, mice, moles, squirrels, and with names such as Prick-ears, Flo, and Bess. Hopkins and his assistant swore in court that they had seen such imps themselves. The witches allegedly performed a variety of *maleficia*: an elderly pastor of Brandeston, John Lowes, was condemned for sinking a ship from Ipswich by magic. Rossell Hope Robbins observes that the judges were so credulous under the influence of Hopkins' persuasion that they made no effort even to 'check whether any ship had foundered that day'.[37] But Hopkins had gone too far too fast. By 1646 considerable opposition to him was already surfacing; later that year he was forced to retire, and the following year he died in some disgrace. In the short space of two years he had earned for himself the informal title of witchfinder-general of England and the contempt of future generations.

The number of witch trials declined rapidly after the excesses of Hopkins and in spite of the continued defence of witch beliefs by learned writers. It is possible that the act of 1604 and the introduction of continental ideas helped speed the end of witchcraft, since they undermined credibility: the common people on the whole did not believe these ideas, and the results of the prosecutions were becoming distasteful to the authorities. The end of the Civil War calmed tensions, and Cromwell's government was not especially interested in suppressing witchcraft.

Learned debate about witch beliefs continued after the Restoration. In 1666 Joseph Glanvill issued *Some Philosophical Considerations Touching Witches and Witchcraft*, a defence of belief in witches on the basis of Christian theology. Denial of witchcraft, he argued, proceeded from atheism. Those who reject witches reject the Devil, and those who reject the Devil reject the entire spirit world, including God himself. But Glanvill's was the last substantial volley from those whom Elliot Rose has called the anti-Sadducees, the learned defenders of witchcraft. John Webster's *Displaying of Supposed Witchcraft* (1677) attacked Glanvill with the argument that belief in God and angels rested on a much firmer theological foundation than belief in witches and could not be compared. Glanvill's work was issued in a greatly expanded version in 1681 under the title *Sadducismus Triumphatus*, 'Sadducism Overcome', but Francis Hutchinson's *Historical Essay Concerning Witchcraft*, published in 1718, was the final devastating blow to witch beliefs. A few learned men may have continued to believe in witchcraft, but they no longer dared say so.

Opposite: frontispiece to Joseph Glanvill's *Sadducismus Triumphatus*, 1681, the last substantial treatise defending belief in witchcraft and attacking witches as a menace to society.

George Cruikshank, *Black John chastising the Witches.* This nineteenth-century satirical sketch was based upon the lurid confessions of Isobel Gowdie in Scotland in 1662.

Trials continued into the Restoration. At Bury St Edmunds in 1662 women were accused and convicted on the testimony of hysterical children, scholars, and because of alleged witches' teats. In Scotland the same year, Isobel Gowdie confessed to a whole catalogue of witch crimes. Isobel confessed voluntarily and without threat of torture, and it is probable that she believed what she was saying; her case is one of the clearest indications that people of unstable mind could under the influence of prevailing beliefs come to believe themselves diabolical witches. It cannot be supposed that she was really the inheritor of an ancient native tradition, because her ideas are strongly continental in flavour and derive from the learned tradition of James I and Glanvill. She claimed that she had met the Devil in church in 1647 and there made a pact with him,

denying Christian baptism, receiving the new name of Janet, the devil's mark on her shoulder, and rebaptism in her own blood which the devil sucked from her. She swore allegiance [to the Devil] by placing one hand on her head and the other on the sole of her foot.[38]

She rode about through the air, changed herself into a jackdaw, a cat, or other forms, and regularly attended a coven of thirteen. What became of Isobel is unknown, but the fame of her trial seems to have penetrated to Somerset, where in 1664 witches were charged with attending covens of thirteen led by a little man in black clothing; they signed a pact, met at night, feasted and danced, and flew through the air with the aid of magical ointments. In 1667

Ursula Clarke of Dunstable was charged with witchcraft in trying to kill William Metcalfe. After a quarrel, she said that he would

> waste like dew against the sun. . . . Some people had wronged her, she said, but they had as good have left her alone, for she . . . had seen the end of Platt, and . . . the end of Haddon, and she hoped she should see the end of Metcalfe, and that she had never wished nor cursed anything in her life but it came to pass.[39]

With Ursula Clarke we have come full circle: back from the catalogue of continental diabolism to plain English cursing and hexing, ever a ready remedy of those who have no power to help or hurt in a natural way.

By the beginning of the eighteenth century, witchcraft was out of fashion among intellectuals, seldom regarded seriously by government prosecutors, and beginning to fade in popular belief. It has been argued that the significant increase in charges of arson and other malicious injury in the period 1686–1712 is the result of a shift in accusations from supernatural to natural crimes. Witch trials practically ceased in the last decades of the seventeenth century, and the last trial for witchcraft in England, that of Jane Wenham in 1731, ended in acquittal. In 1736, the statute of 1604 was repealed. But meanwhile, English witchcraft put on one last important show, not in England itself, but in the American colonies.

WITCHCRAFT IN THE AMERICAN COLONIES

America was culturally behind the mother country. Witchcraft had become a serious problem in England by the 1560s, but it was not till the 1640s that New England began to suffer. The first hanging of a witch in New England occurred in Connecticut in 1647; a number of other cases came to court in the 1640s to 1680s, and there were hangings at Providence in 1662. The intellectual leaders of New England defended belief in witches. Cotton Mather's *Memorable Providences Relating to Witchcraft and Possessions* (1689) and *Wonders of the Invisible World* (1693) both upheld the tradition. The most memorable and well-documented trials for witchcraft in America occurred at Salem in 1692. Both intellectual and legal precedents had prepared New Englanders to believe in witchcraft, and a number of social and political tensions existed in Massachusetts and particularly in Salem that inclined people to lodge accusations and to believe in them. The immediate cause of the frenzy was the occult activity of some children in Salem Village.

Two small girls aged nine and eleven began experimenting with divination in a half-serious attempt to discover who their future husbands would be. As often happens with people who play with magic, the children became terrified and began to exhibit nervous symptoms, thrashing about and assuming odd postures. The father of one of the girls was Samuel Parris, the minister of Salem Village. Parris called in a physician, but the doctor, unable to discern any physical cause, suggested to Mr Parris that the children might be the victims of a witch's spell. The girls' behaviour became worse, and now a number of other girls and young women began to suffer (or enjoy) fits and convulsions. These others may have been overcome by the power of unconscious suggestion. Or they may have enjoyed the attention they

Cotton Mather. Cotton Mather's theological writings encouraged belief in witchcraft, and during the Salem trials he did not lift a finger to help the accused.

received, or the excitement of it all, or the bizarre behaviour that they were permitted to display on the assumption that they were bewitched: one daughter of a strict and pious father hurled the family Bible across the room; another pulled brands from the hearth and ran about shouting gibberish at the top of her voice. For some the spell may have been a delusion, for others a malicious prank. In the end, it cost nineteen people their lives.

The girls were subjected to intense questioning by adults and under pressure accused three women, Sarah Goode, Sarah Osborne, and a West Indian slave named Tituba, of bewitching them. Osborne and Goode denied the charges, but Tituba confessed with great gusto, declaring that she had commerce with the Devil as a 'thing all over hairy, all the face hairy, and a long nose'.[40] Tituba's motives for confessing are unclear, but her confession lent terror and panic to an already tense situation. The irony is that her confession may have saved her. None who confessed to witchcraft was hanged, for the girls always reported an amelioration of their symptoms after a confession, but many who denied the charges were hanged, often after the girls' symptoms had worsened at their trials.

Under pressure, threat, and suggestion the accusations grew. They followed the English tradition rather than the continental: the Devil apparently modified his behaviour according to national preferences. The witches frequented a secret society where the Devil appeared as a black man and baptized them in his name. They partook of an evil, black communion bread; they harboured demons in the forms of animals and suckled them with blood through their witches' teats, and they performed *maleficia* against their enemies, causing illness, moving objects supernaturally and, of course, tormenting the afflicted girls with fits and convulsions.

The fits continued to increase in intensity as time went on. The girls screeched and howled, reported visions of ghosts and imps, and suffered mysterious teeth-marks on their arms. The fear of witchcraft spread from Salem Village to Salem Town; learned clergymen in Boston debated the events, and one accused witch was arrested as far away as Maine and brought back to stand trial. As fear swelled, adults began to experience some of the hysterical symptoms themselves. A fourth witch – Martha Cory – was named, and when she appeared for interrogation in the village meeting-house, the possessed girls became uncontrollably agitated.

When she wrung her hands, they screamed that they were being pinched; when she bit her lips, they declared that they could feel teeth biting their own flesh.[41]

More witches were accused, but trials had to wait until the new governor of the colony, Sir William Phips, arrived with a new charter. Meanwhile, Cotton Mather and other Massachusetts ministers met in June to urge both vigorous prosecution of witches and caution in passing judgment. Mather warned that though witchcraft was a serious problem, it was difficult to determine who was a witch, and innocent people might be destroyed by hasty action.

Unfortunately the ministers took no action at all as the trials progressed. Phips arrived and authorized the commencement of the trials. The first hanging occurred on 10 June 1692. Five more witches were hanged on 19

July including Sarah Goode, and six more on 5 August. Far from attempting to stop the killings, Cotton Mather appeared at the scaffold during George Burroughs' execution, and when Burroughs shook the confidence of the assembly by reciting the Lord's Prayer fervently and perfectly, Mather gave a spirited impromptu speech urging that the execution continue. By the time of the final execution for witchcraft on 22 September 1692, nineteen persons had been executed and more than a hundred jailed. It had been a summer of horror begun by hysterical or malicious girls and in one sense ended by them: the girls were present at that last execution in September to taunt the victims as they awaited their deaths on the scaffold.

But now, as in Europe, the terrible toll taken by the craze generated a backlash of public opinion. At last the ministers spoke out. Cotton Mather's father, Increase Mather, gave a sermon in colonial Cambridge, arguing that 'it were better that ten suspected witches should escape, than that one innocent person should be condemned.'[42] Mather severely criticized the use of evidence in the trials, arguing that much of it had been suspect. His chief concern was that 'the evil deeds on which the indictments rested were not physically perpetrated by the witches at all, but by intangible spirits who could at times assume their shape.'[43]

Paul Boyer and Stephen Nissenbaum describe in their book on the Salem witchcraft the three main types of evidence provided at the trials. The first was direct confession, which was often supported by corroborating detail. In continental courts, confessions were often obtained through torture, but following English law torture was used in Salem only when the accused refused to enter any kind of plea. However, confessions were encouraged by terror, suggestion, and sometimes severe physical persuasions amounting almost to torture, such as enforced sleeplessness.

A second variety of evidence was empirical proof of the witch's use of supernatural power. The witch might demonstrate supernatural strength: George Burroughs allegedly could lift enormously heavy weights. Or the witch might be unable to recite his prayers correctly: one poor wretch met his doom by saying 'hollowed be thy name' while reciting the Lord's Prayer. Or, of course, the witches might on examination be found to possess a devil's mark or witch's teat on their bodies. Anger on the part of a witch followed by trouble on the part of her victim was another such empirical demonstration. John Willard, accused of witchcraft, went in his distress to ask old Bray Williams for his prayers. Bray refused, and when he next encountered John he thought that he received a piercing glance. Immediately afterwards he found that he was unable to pass water, and a few days afterwards a young kinsman met an unexpected death. Upon Willard's conviction and execution, Bray Williams happily regained full use of his bladder. On her way to trial, Bridget Bishop cast her gaze on a meeting-house, whereupon a roof-beam crashed to the floor. Increase Mather was unwilling to admit such evidence as convincing, but the courts were more generous.

Mather was particularly opposed to the use of 'spectral evidence', and here again the courts proved more credulous. Many of the witnesses claimed to have seen demons manifest themselves as spectres visible only to the witness and not to others present at the same time. A 'short, dark man' might appear,

Opposite: frontispiece to Increase Mather's account of the Salem witch trials. Unlike his son Cotton, Increase worked to bring the witch-craze in Massachusetts under control.

A FURTHER
ACCOUNT
OF THE
TRYALS
OF THE
New-England Witches.

WITH THE
OBSERVATIONS
Of a Person who was upon the Place several
Days when the suspected Witches were
first taken into Examination.

To which is added,

Cases of Conscience
Concerning Witchcrafts and Evil Spirits Per-
sonating Men.

Written at the Request of the Ministers of New-England.

By Increase Mather, President of Harvard Colledge.

Licensed and Entred according to Order.

London: Printed for J. Dunton, at the Raven in the Poultrey
1693. Of whom may be had the Third Edition of Mr. Cotton
Mather's First Account of the Tryals of the New-England
Witches, Printed on the same size with this Last Account,
that they may bind up together.

or a 'gray cat'. Typically the witness would see the spectre and call out to a companion; the companion would see nothing; he would strike at the place with a weapon, and the witness would see the spectre's coat torn or some other effect of the blow. Mather argued that there could be no corroboration of such evidence and that it should therefore not be admitted, but again the courts had been more tolerant. The faultiness of such evidence was obvious to most open-minded people, and its use by the courts one of the elements undermining public confidence in the trials.

Had there been any truth at all in the accusations? The sources for the trials are extraordinarily full, so that they constitute the test case for the existence of witchcraft in America. The most credulous modern historian of witchcraft, Montague Summers, argued that most of the accused were innocent but that a few seem really to have been members of a secret group. For this assertion there is no reliable evidence at all. It is possible that some of the accused may have mumbled curses at their enemies and conceivable that one or two may have done so with intent to work malicious magic. It is also possible that the slave Tituba, who confessed so readily and freely, practised some kind of magic and believed that she had communed with the Devil, but of all the interrogations and trials, Tituba's is the only one that suggests this. The rest of the evidence is drawn from the traditions of English witchcraft so fully elucidated by Cotton Mather and the other intellectual leaders of the colony. It cannot of course be demonstrated conclusively that no coven of witches existed at Salem, but the evidence all points in the other direction. The antics of a group of silly girls, in the right (or wrong) social circumstances, and with an intellectual tradition of witch beliefs to hand, plunged the colony of Massachusetts into a late, but severe, manifestation of the witch-craze.

The history of witchcraft is the investigation of a concept; it is also an attempt to understand the social conditions and interactions that encouraged the development of the concept. In the past ten years, most historians have emphasized the social history of witchcraft, an emphasis that has both virtues and limitations. The chief virtue is the recognition that ideas do not develop in a vacuum and that social relationships do much to shape perceptions of reality. The second virtue is thoroughness. Macfarlane, Midelfort, Monter, and Boyer and Nissenbaum have concentrated upon narrow segments of space and time and examined these microcosms in as sophisticated a manner as the data permit. The chief dangers of the approach are that it has tended to be dogmatic, blocking or dismissing other approaches, and that in its search for the social mechanisms of witchcraft it misses the broader ethical, intellectual, and spiritual meaning of witchcraft.

One kind of insight provided by social historians is that witchcraft or witch beliefs performed a social function. Sometimes the function was conscious and cynical, as when Henry VIII accused Anne Boleyn of practising witchcraft in order to seduce him, or when the inquisitors plotted to arrest rich men and confiscate their goods. Much more frequently, the function was the unconscious need to blame someone for the misfortunes of daily life. If you are impotent, it is less embarrassing and better for your self-image if you can place the blame on a sorcerer. If your cow dies, or you fall ill with dysentery, it is more prudent to blame a witch than to blame God. Witchcraft shifts blame for misfortune from an abstract and inscrutable force to an identifiable, punishable individual. If God, or fate, has caused your illness, you have no means of fighting back, but if a witch is responsible, you may be able to fend her off or break her power. If you can have her arrested, tried, and executed, her power over you will fail, and your good fortune will return. This belief helps explain the large number of executions; killing the witch is the only way to make sure that she cannot return to exact magical revenge. As in Africa a person may be genuinely helped by a witch-doctor, so the European evidence suggests that witch trials had a genuine therapeutic effect on the alleged victims.

Another important function of witchcraft was the same as that of heresy: to define the boundaries of Christianity and achieve the cohesion of the Christian community in the face of a terrifying and powerful army of foes under the generalship of Satan himself.

Social historians have investigated the correlations between witchcraft and other social phenomena. In spite of caricatures of the witch as an ugly old hag, physical appearance was not a common ground for accusations of

Witches offer a child to the Devil. More susceptible to disease and irrational fears than adults, and less sensitive to the pain that accusations could cause, children were often the catalysts for charges of witchcraft.

witchcraft. The most decisive traits tending to draw witch charges were begging, grumbling, cursing, and quarrelling. Witches were of all ages, though in Essex the commonest age category was fifty to sixty years old, possibly because age was supposed to enhance magical wisdom. Though children were frequently possessed, they were seldom accused of witchcraft themselves. Much more frequently they were the alleged victims of witchcraft, becoming accusers or at least the catalysts for accusations. The cases of the Burton Boy (1596), the Bilson Boy (1620), the Throgmorton Girls (1688), the Goodwin Children (1688), and of course the Salem girls (1692), are examples of the many accusations growing out of the alleged bewitchment of children. This is not surprising. Children were more susceptible both to disease and to irrational fears; they caused mischief and antagonized neighbours; they were perceived as vulnerable to attack, and above all they were less sensitive than adults to the pain that accusations would bring to others.

Psychologists have investigated the state of mind in which a person might believe in her own powers as a witch, but historians have found no convincing correlation between witchcraft and mental illness on the part of either accusers or accused. The concept of individual psychopathology is not helpful when an entire society embraces a delusion. An educated Englishman or American who today believed that Jews were engineering the troubles of the world would probably have an individual psychological problem; a German believing this in 1940 might well be merely adopting the common beliefs of his society. Most individuals believing in witchcraft in 1600 were neither stupid nor mad, though their society may have been both.

In Essex, Alan Macfarlane found no correlation between the incidence of illness and witch accusations. 'Concurrently with the years of fiercest prosecution, many people died sudden deaths which were not blamed on witches.' This was true even of a plague of infant mortality. No specific diseases were blamed on witchcraft, though lingering illnesses were more likely to be attributed to witchcraft than sudden attacks. Macfarlane argues that the nature of the illness itself was not important, but rather the victim's perception of the meaning of misfortune. 'The social relationship of the victim, rather than the . . . nature of the illness . . . determined a person's reaction to misfortune.' To explain the rise and decline of the witch-craze, therefore, we need to look less at the troubles society faces, whether illness, famine, and war, than at 'the social relationships which determine the way in which people react to misfortune.'[44] Thus efforts to tie witchcraft to the enclosure movement in England or the Thirty Years War in Germany may lead to little more than a vague generalization that people are more prone to make negative psychological projections when times are bad.

Midelfort observed, however, that the incidence of witch trials could increase significantly after a natural disaster. At Balingen, for example, the destruction of a large part of the town by fire was followed by the arrest of three women for witchcraft. The prime suspect was tortured, released after the evidence against her was found to be insufficient, but then attacked on the street by a mob, which stoned her to death. Fires and other disasters raise people's fears and increase the likelihood of their seeking scapegoats. But fires often occur without being followed by witch accusations, and witch accusations often occur in the absence of any disaster. Disaster is a contributing element, but disaster produces witch accusations only when certain world beliefs predominate, and the presence of such beliefs depends in turn upon certain social and intellectual conditions.

Correlations between witchcraft and social class are inconclusive. In southwestern Germany both rich and poor were accused, and there was a fairly even distribution of wealth among those convicted. In England, witches were on the whole marginally poorer than their victims, the witches coming mainly from the labouring classes and the victims mainly from the yeoman class. The Caroline Code in Germany forbade the indiscriminate use of confiscation. Despite some gross exceptions, the desire to confiscate property was not among the important motives of the witch-craze. Nor did declining economic conditions necessarily correlate with witchcraft. Macfarlane observed that in Essex prosecutions were at their height in the 1580s and 1590s, a period of relative prosperity.

The firmest generalization coming out of the study of southwestern Germany was that the two groups most susceptible to accusation were people of unusually bad reputation and people of unusually good reputation.

Thieves, sex offenders, brawlers, midwives (unfortunately but inevitably these had a bad reputation), and quarrellers were likely to be accused. On the other hand, magistrates, merchants, and teachers were also likely to be accused, though the nobility, physicians (oddly), lawyers, and students were not. People who in any way stood out from the crowd were more vulnerable. In a large witch panic the pattern would be something like this: individuals would lodge accusations against an unpopular person such as a midwife. Once the trial began, the witch would implicate other people under torture, and these would tend to be those she knew personally for good or ill: family, acquaintances, or enemies. Witch trials often involved a whole family for this reason, and sometimes mothers and daughters were executed together. Eight members of one German family were executed for witchcraft between November 1628 and June 1630. Through malice, fear, and threat of torture, accusations would spread, and finally the whole community would be involved.

One hypothetical cause of the witch-craze was the rapidly changing demography of the period between the mid-fourteenth and sixteenth centuries, especially the movement from the countryside into the city. In manorial society, a small, tight community was strictly regulated by tradition and custom and by the authority of the manorial lord and his officials. The opinions and judgments of elders, neighbours, the priest, and the lord's representatives weighed heavily, and there was little sense of isolation. Local courts easily controlled most of the social problems that did arise. When people moved from this settled community life to the city, they experienced a cultural shock similar to that produced in Africa when tribal structure was broken down owing to urbanization. In both continents, traditional patterns of kinship and community shifted, leaving individuals insecure as to their duties towards others and the duties of others towards them. Under such conditions fear of witchcraft increased. There is little evidence, however, to indicate that people new to the urban community were more likely to be accused than the more established inhabitants.

In the countryside, accusations commonly arose among neighbours; ordinarily the alleged witch resented her victim for some real or imagined lack of charity or neighbourliness, such as failure to invite her to a party or to help her when she was in need. In some cases the witch would practise magic in order to retaliate. Or those who had injured her, feeling guilty, would project their guilt and anger on to her and blame her for a subsequent misfortune. At Chelmsford in 1579 Margery Stanton was accused of witchcraft by several neighbours who had refused to give her charity and had subsequently suffered illness, the death of cattle, and other misfortunes. In Lucerne, the child of Dorothea Hindremstein had a fight with another boy. Dorothea told the other boy that he would never forget what he had done, and later that day he developed a swelling and lay ill for weeks. Dorothea was accused of witchcraft. In Todi, Italy, a girl contracted a disease after having an affair with a married man, and the wife was subsequently accused of bewitching her!

This pattern of individual hostility and accusation, typical of most continental witchcraft before the fifteenth century, remained common in

England until the eighteenth century. During the height of the witch-craze, the pattern changed on the continent, and witches were perceived as part of a vast plot against Christian society. This was especially true in France, the Low Countries, Germany, and the Alpine regions. The explanation for the intensity of the craze in those areas lies in the strong tradition of heresy, the standardization of interrogations by the inquisition, and the disruption brought about by religious wars.

WITCHCRAFT AND WOMEN

The most marked social correlation is that between witchcraft and women. Over the entire course of the witch-craze at least twice as many women were accused as men. Variations in time and geography occurred: in southwestern Germany, for example, more men were accused after 1620 than before, and children were commonly accused after 1627. But this means only that the predominance of women was somewhat less than it had been. Women dominated witchcraft in every period and in every region. The stereotype of the witch is still so powerful that most people are surprised to learn that male witches exist at all or else suppose that the male counterpart of a witch is a 'warlock'. If someone is called 'an ugly witch', the gender is never in doubt.

What is the reason for this sexism, chauvinism, or – more accurately – misogyny? Midelfort observed that the sixteenth century tended to be unusually misogynistic, possibly because demographic changes produced a larger number of women living alone than usual. Marriages occurred later in life, and a greater proportion of people never married. The Reformation brought the dissolution of convents, and even in Catholic regions the number of women in convents declined. If, as Midelfort estimates, perhaps 20 per cent of women never married, and between 10 and 20 per cent were widows, then something like 40 per cent of women may have lived without the legal and social protection of husbands. Many unmarried women and widows found a home with brothers, sons, or others, but the proportion of single and lonely women seems to have increased. Such persons, isolated, unhappy, impoverished, and grumbling, were easy targets for accusations of witchcraft. Such problems, possibly greatest in the sixteenth century, existed throughout the entire span of the witch-craze.

Women living without the patriarchal family support of father and husband had little influence and little legal and social redress for wrongs. They had to do what they could. Since they were barred from normally effective means, they had recourse to means typically employed by powerless people. Arson, for example, was frequently attributed to old women, since it is a crime that can be perpetrated by a weak person clandestinely. In a society that took magic seriously, spells and curses formed another obvious category of response. Once this kind of crime was associated with lonely women, no lonely woman could be free of suspicion. An angry glare would be interpreted as the evil eye, an irate epithet as a curse, muttering as invocation, and loitering as working a spell. Old men also ran this kind of risk, but widows almost always outnumbered widowers. Women tend to live longer, and did then, providing they survived childbirth. During the plagues

women survived much more readily, in some places having a recovery rate at least 600 per cent higher than that of males. Under the stress and fear that accompanied the plagues, it was common to suspect the women of using magic to ensure their survival or even of encompassing the deaths of the men. The very weakness of the social position of women, particularly widows or unmarried women, made it safer to accuse them than to accuse men, whose political, financial, legal, and even physical strength rendered the accuser more liable to reprisals. A physically weak, socially isolated, financially destitute, and legally powerless old woman could offer only the deterrent of her spells.

Childbirth, with its dangers to both mother and infant, was commonly attended by a midwife, and the death, deformity, and other calamities that might occur were often laid at her door, as we have seen. Husbands felt guilt and anger at the death of wife or child and readily projected these feelings upon the midwife, who was charged with negligence or, if no physical reason for the disaster could be found, with sorcery.

The connection of witchcraft with heresy encouraged the emphasis upon women. Historians have long observed that women were more influential in heresy than in other aspects of medieval society. Women, finding themselves prevented from rising to positions of influence in the establishment, turned to heresy instead. The Waldensians, for example, allowed women to preach, and the Catharists admitted them to the ranks of the *perfecti*. The relative importance of women in heresy and in heresy trials transferred readily to witchcraft and witch trials.

The misogyny that appeared in such virulent form during the witch-craze had an age-old tradition behind it. Most societies have placed women in an inferior position, and the misogyny of Western civilization was fed by at least three sources: the Classical literary tradition, Hebrew religion, and dualism. In the Classical literary tradition women's roles reflected their actual status in Greek and Roman society: that is, as subservient to men. Women do not usually play an important role in Classical literature – Creusas are more common than Didos. When they do, it is often as almost passive catalysts of ruin, such as Helen of Troy. Even when they are active, it is more for ill than for good, witness Circe, Medea, and Clytemnestra. And, as with Circe and Medea again, the evil deeds of women are often perceived as black sorcery.

Hebrew religion, more than the other religions of the ancient Near East, placed women in a distinctly inferior position. Ancient misogyny was reinforced by the dualist belief in a struggle pitting the body and evil against the spirit and good. Theoretically this dualism condemns the carnality of men as much as that of women, but society was dominated by men, who projected their lusts upon women and made them responsible for carnality. Thus Eve became the prototypical sensual seductress.

Christianity affirmed the spiritual equality of men and women, but St Paul and many of the most influential Church Fathers blurred that doctrine. Women became the temptresses of men, men who moved the wheels of state, of religion, and of learning, men whose souls were practically, if not theoretically, more important. In most Christian theology and tradition this misogyny was kept within bounds, but sometimes it burst out crudely.

Opposite: Goya, *The Sabbat, c.* 1794–5. Witches were invariably thought of as female, and Goya's vision of the goat-Devil among his worshippers is no exception.

Heinrich Institoris, the author of the *Malleus Maleficarum*, spoke from this position when he explained the predominance of women in witchcraft:

What else is woman but a foe to friendship, an inescapable punishment, a necessary evil, a natural temptation, a desirable calamity, a domestic danger, a delectable detriment, an evil of nature, painted in fair colours. . . . The word woman is used to mean the lust of the flesh, as it is said: I have found a woman more bitter than death, and a good woman more subject to carnal lust. . . . [Women] are more credulous; and since the chief aim of the devil is to corrupt faith, therefore he rather attacks them [than men]. . . . Women are naturally more impressionable. . . . They have slippery tongues, and are unable to conceal from their fellow-women those things which by evil arts they know. . . . Women are intellectually like children. . . . She is more carnal than a man, as is clear from her many carnal abominations. . . . She is an imperfect animal, she always deceives. . . . Therefore a wicked woman is by her nature quicker to waver in her faith, and consequently quicker to abjure the faith, which is the root of witchcraft. . . . Just as through the first defect in their intelligence they are more prone to abjure the faith; so through their second defect of inordinate affections and passions they search for, brood over, and inflict various vengeances, either by witchcraft, or by some other means. . . . Women also have weak memories; and it is a natural vice in them not to be disciplined, but to follow their own impulses without any sense of what is due. . . . She is a liar by nature. . . . Let us also consider her gait, posture, and habit, in which is vanity of vanities.[45]

We may not wish to hear more, but Institoris' contemporaries did. The powerful influence of the *Malleus* was due in large part to its resonance with the dualist and misogynist tradition deeply inherent in Christianity. Far from bringing any relief, the Protestant Reformation, with its return to the primitive Christianity of the apostles and fathers, emphasized mistrust of women even more than did the Catholic Church. Luther's writings writhe with fear of women.

To blame Christianity and Judaism alone for misogyny would be to miss the point. The Judaeo-Christian tradition of monotheism expelled the feminine principle from the Deity. Yet in fact the social position of women was often clearly inferior in polytheistic religions. And Christianity was much more enlightened than its contemporary rivals. Mithraism, Christianity's chief competitor for influence in the early Roman Empire, denied women salvation and even entry into the temple. The terror of women, the belief that they work dark and mysterious deeds, is an ancient, almost universal phenomenon in men, and must thus be understood in terms of the history of the male unconscious.

Jung and others who have studied the symbolism of the feminine comment on its powerful ambivalence. Male domination of religion, literature, and law created a special symbolism and mythology about women characterized by a tripartite ambivalence. Woman is the pure virgin; woman is the kindly mother; woman is the vicious and carnal hag. In Greek religion, the goddess Artemis was the virgin sister of Apollo, she was the patroness of childbirth and the guarantor of the fertility of animals, and she was also Hecate, the underworld goddess of witchcraft and spells. Christianity traditionally found it difficult to accept the principle of ambivalence in the deity: the Christian God was wholly good and wholly masculine, excluding

Opposite: frontispiece to Heinrich Institoris' *Malleus Maleficarum*, 'The Hammer of Witches'. First published in 1486, the *Malleus* was frequently reprinted, became enormously popular, and helped initiate the witch-craze.

MALLEVS

MALEFICARVM,

MALEFICAS ET EARVM

haeresim frameâ conterens,

EX VARIIS AVCTORIBVS COMPILATVS,
& in quatuor Tomos iustè distributus,

*QVORVM DVO PRIORES VANAS DÆMONVM
versutias, præstigiosas eorum delusiones, superstitiosas Strigimagarum
cæremonias, horrendos etiam cum illis congressus ; exactam denique
tam pestiferæ sectæ disquisitionem, & punitionem complectuntur.
Tertius praxim Exorcistarum ad Dæmonum, & Strigimagarum maleficia de Christi fidelibus pellenda ; Quartus verò Artem Doctrinalem,
Benedictionalem, & Exorcismalem continent.*

TOMVS PRIMVS.

Indices Auctorum, capitum, rerúmque non desunt.

Editio nouissima, infinitis penè mendis expurgata ; cuique accessit Fuga
Dæmonum & Complementum artis exorcisticæ.

Vir siue mulier, in quibus Pythonicus, vel diuinationis fuerit spiritus, morte moriatur ;
Leuitici cap. 10.

LVGDVNI,

Sumptibus Claudii Bourgeat, sub signo Mercurij Galli.

M. DC. LXIX.

both the feminine principle and the principle of evil. Repression of the principle of evil from the godhead led to the development of the concept of the Devil. Repression of the feminine principle produced a new ambivalence of idealization and contempt.

Beginning in the twelfth century, a new idealization of the female began. One manifestation of this idealization was courtly love. Courtly love was in large part a literary device, it applied only to aristocrats, and it had nothing to do with practical equality. But it did elevate the lady of high birth to an idealized position of moral superiority over the male.

The second manifestation was the cult of the Blessed Virgin Mary. Though always venerated in the early church, the Virgin was not at first an unusually important saint. But from the twelfth century onwards the cult of the Virgin flourished all over Europe. It was rejected by the Protestants but still remains powerful in the Roman Catholic Church today. The cult of the Virgin was a limited and unconscious effort to bring the feminine principle back into the concept of the deity, and its current decline in Christianity may be seen as a step backwards.

But the idealization of woman had an opposite effect. Whenever any one principle is exaggerated, it tends to create a shadow, a mirror-image, an opposite principle. The exaggeration of the goodness and purity of the female in courtly love and the cult of the Virgin created the shadow-image of the hag. The Virgin Mother of God incarnated two points of the ancient threefold symbolism of the female: the virgin and the mother. But Christianity repressed the third point, the dark spirit of night and the underworld. This dark side of the feminine principle did not disappear: rather, as the power of the Virgin Mother grew, so did the power of the hag. In ancient religion, the dark side had been integrated with the light side, but now, entirely cut off from the positive side of the female principle and repressed, the hag became totally evil. A further transformation occurred. In ancient religions, the hag was a manifestation of a spiritual being, a goddess or at least a demon. But now, in Christian Europe, the hag image was projected upon human beings. The European witch, then, must be understood not just as a sorceress, but as the incarnation of the hag. She is a totally evil and depraved person under the domination and command of Satan.

The Salem trials

These are some of the macrocosmic notions of the social origins of witchcraft. In microcosm, the Salem trials provide a well-documented example of the social mechanisms of witchcraft at a local level. The recent study of Salem by Boyer and Nissenbaum properly treats the history of witchcraft in Massachusetts in the context of other social movements in the colony. The behaviour of the young girls claiming to be victims was not dissimilar to behaviour noted during the religious revival at colonial Northampton in 1734-5. 'With a slight shift in the mix of social ingredients, [Salem and Boston] could have fostered scenes of religious questing in 1692', instead of scenes of witchcraft.[46] In both the religious revival and in witchcraft, young

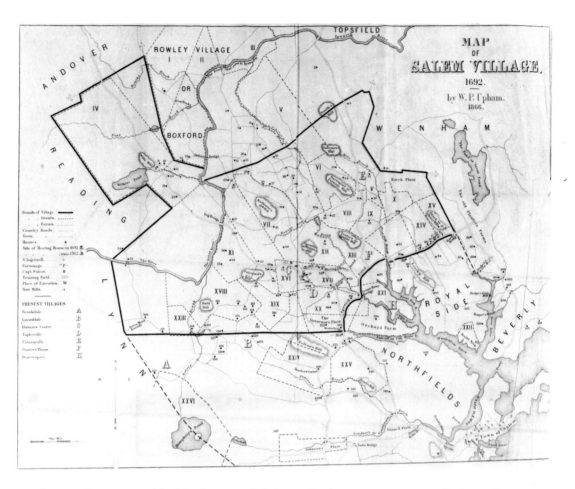

Map of Salem Village in
1692, the year of the witch-
craze.

people were dominant and had broken out of their usual subservient and
deferential social role. In both instances too the ministers exploited the bizarre
behaviour of the young people in order to bolster their own slipping
leadership. What then produced witchcraft in the one instance and revival in
the other? Primarily the difference in intellectual preconception, the
'interpretation which the adult leadership of each community placed upon
physical and mental states which in themselves were strikingly similar.'[47] In
Northampton distraught emotional states were seen as the descent of the
Holy Spirit, in Salem as an assault by Satan. This observation by
Boyer and Nissenbaum confirms those of Midelfort and Monter in Europe:
natural and social disasters cannot in themselves explain the incidence of
witchcraft; it was the magical explanations people placed upon the disasters
that caused them to blame witches. A sophisticated social history of
witchcraft will give full weight to the history of concepts and avoid simplistic
correlations between external phenomena and witch beliefs.

Boyer and Nissenbaum point to the importance of local geography in the
Salem craze. Most of the accusers lived on the west side of Salem Village;
most of the accused and those who supported them lived on the east side. The
uncertain legal status of Salem Village (as opposed to Salem Town) had

caused political disputes and hard feelings. The most important source of unhappiness was James Bayley, the first minister appointed to Salem Village (1679). Bayley was a controversial individual, and the dispute centring on him broadened until it included the whole question of the governance of the church, especially the question of who had the right to hire and dismiss ministers. What made these disputes over Salem Village Church so destructive was the fact that the constitution of the church was so ill defined that the community had no structured way of dealing with disputes and resorted instead to vituperation. This situation, peculiar to Salem Village at least in degree, may explain why the craze was more powerful there than elsewhere. The constitutional disputes attending the overthrow of King James II in 1688–9 also contributed by weakening the authority of the British and colonial governments as well as provoking political dissension in the village. Further, the political relationship between Salem Village and Salem Town was ill defined. The Village resented both its dependence on the Town and the Town's failure to exercise its authority to maintain tranquillity.

In 1689, at the height of the constitutional crisis in London, a new minister, Samuel Parris, was appointed. The village quickly divided into supporters and opponents of Parris. This struggle was exacerbated by taking on a moral aspect, as was typical of Puritan society. The Puritans could not perceive the conflict as merely personal, or political or economic, or even constitutional. They saw it as a 'mortal conflict involving the very nature of the community'.[48] Boyer and Nissenbaum observe that 'the witchcraft episode did not generate the divisions within the Village, nor did it shift them in any fundamental way, but it laid bare the intensity with which they were experienced and heightened the vindictiveness with which they were expressed.'[49] Thus the witchcraft outbreak was the violent expression of deeply felt moral divisions, the moral divisions were generated by the quarrel over the governance of the church, and the quarrel over the governance of the church was exacerbated by strongly felt neighbourhood and family problems. Hostility would have been expressed one way or another, but the existence of the tradition of witchcraft made it a natural vehicle for these angers.

The problems of the Putnam family illustrate the process. The mother died, and the father remarried. The children of the first marriage felt deep resentment towards their stepmother and her son. They projected their bitterness towards their stepmother upon other persons politically or psychologically less threatening to them, notably vulnerable women of the stepmother's generation. The family supported the ministry of Samuel Parris and identified the resentment they felt toward Parris' enemies with the resentment they felt towards their stepmother. Those whom they identified with their stepmother they also identified as opponents of Parris; opponents of Parris were morally reprehensible; the old women were therefore part of an evil conspiracy against Parris.

Such ideas were encouraged by Parris himself. 'He took the nagging fears and conflicting impulses of his hearers and wove them into a pattern overwhelming in its scope, a universal drama in which Christ and Satan, Heaven and Hell, struggled for supremacy.'[50] Personal enemies had been

transformed into enemies of the community and enemies of the community into servants of Satan.

Given the existence of the tradition of witchcraft, the possibility that these tensions would be converted into a witch-craze was strong. Then, in 1690–92, a number of unpredictable circumstances came together as the immediate causes of the outbreak. Samuel Parris had a West Indian slave steeped in magical lore; a number of adolescent girls, related to Parris or connected with his political faction, began to dabble in divination and the occult; the Putnam family dispute came to a head; ·the political and constitutional weakness of the government severely limited its ability to control the situation in Salem Village. The supporters of the minister took the lurid accusations of the hysterical girls as confirmation of what they already suspected: their opponents were evil; they were the willing servants of Satan. Parris' opponents had been transformed into witches, and could now be tortured and hanged.

As Trevor-Roper observed of the witch-craze in general, once a 'great fear' takes hold of society, 'that society looks naturally to the stereotype of the enemy in its midst; and once the witch had become the stereotype, witchcraft would be the universal accusation.[51] Fortunately, Salem was the last major witch trial in the English-speaking world, and even on the continent the craze had by 1700 begun to wane.

The trial of George Jacobs, Salem, 1692, showing the hysterical atmosphere of the courtroom. Jacobs was hanged on the testimony of his granddaughter, Margaret Jacobs, who later admitted her accusations were false.

7 The decline of witchcraft

The witch-craze began to decline by the middle of the seventeenth century, but popular opinion, conservative intellectuals, and obstinate judges prolonged it, sometimes against the will and command of government, which increasingly perceived it as disruptive to social order. The delusion persisted longer in Protestant countries than in Catholic, possibly because of the influence of the conservative pietism typical of popular Protestantism at the time. It also lingered in outlying areas after it had begun to fade in cultural centres. This was true in the larger sense – witchcraft reached its height in America and Scandinavia late in the seventeenth century – and in the smaller sense: witchcraft persisted in the countryside longer than in the cities. Sweden's most spectacular trial occurred in 1669 in the town of Mora. A number of children of Mora claimed that they had been carried by witches to a place called Blocula, where witches held a sabbat presided over by Satan. Most of the traditional elements of continental witch belief were introduced at the trial, many of the accused were scourged, and eighty-five were burnt.

The notoriety of such trials as Salem and Mora helped turn opinion against witch beliefs. The cultural and political leaders of Europe gradually abandoned their support and exerted their influence to end the craze. The decline was continuous, and the prosecution of witches virtually ceased by the middle of the eighteenth century. The last execution for witchcraft in England occurred in 1684, in America 1692, in Scotland 1727, in France 1745, and in Germany 1775.

The legal decline of witchcraft in Britain was gradual but steady. In 1684 Alice Molland was executed for witchcraft at Exeter. It was almost thirty years before the next conviction, that of Jane Wenham in 1712, and she was pardoned and released. In 1717 Jane Clerk was indicted for witchcraft, but the case was dismissed. In 1736 a statute repealed the statutes of Mary of Scotland (1562), Elizabeth I (1563), and James I and VI (1604), stating that 'no prosecution, suit or proceeding shall be commenced or carried out against any person or persons for witchcraft, sorcery, inchantment [sic], or conjuration.' The statute of 1736 continued to provide for prosecution of those pretending to possess magical powers, but it denied reality to those powers. It remained the law until 1951, when it was replaced by the even more liberal Fraudulent Mediums Act, although in 1963 a demand for the reinstatement of the witchcraft laws was made, owing to the desecration of churches and graveyards, which the supporters of the demand supposed, rightly or wrongly, to have been carried out by witches. The statute of 1736 and comparable laws in other countries marked the end of official prosecution for witchcraft.

Burning of the witches of Mora in 1670, one of the last manifestations of the witch-craze in Europe.

The same legal, intellectual, and religious élites that had initiated and fomented the witch-craze now slowly brought it to a halt. Belief in witchcraft and sorcery no longer had their stamp of approval. Only after the governing élites had rejected witch beliefs did popular support wither away. Belief in diabolical Satanic witchcraft declined rapidly in the eighteenth century, virtually disappearing save in legend, literature, and jest. On the other hand, belief in simple sorcery continued right through the eighteenth and nineteenth centuries and on into the present. The union between diabolical witchcraft and sorcery was temporary, and it was artificially engineered by intellectuals rather than rising from folk beliefs. Simple sorcery existed before the witch-craze, during the witch-craze, and after the witch-craze; and it still exists today. Diabolical witchcraft was invented in the Middle Ages, flourished between 1450 and 1650, and then declined and fell. The collapse of the witch-craze between 1650 and 1750 was brought about by a combination of intellectual, pragmatic, and social changes.

Throughout the witch-craze there had been sceptics to write and speak against it, but their influence was limited by the fear of prosecution and by the powerful intellectual pressures exerted by the prevailing belief-system. To reject witchcraft was to court persecution or mockery. No intellectual framework existed from which to fight witchcraft beliefs. The sceptics based their arguments on common sense, on charity, on mercy, or on references to ancient documents such as the Canon Episcopi. But they were still arguing from within the same traditional Christian framework as the witch-hunters. This is why the Protestant Reformation did nothing at all to ameliorate the craze. So long as it was accepted that the Devil exerts great power in the world for the purpose of thwarting the saving mission of Christ, and that organized groups of heretics are plotting against Christian society, then the transposition of heretics into Devil-worshippers was easy and natural. One could argue that this or that heretic was not really a witch, or that flights through the air did not really occur, or that the measures taken against this or that accused witch were too harsh, but one could not challenge the heart of the belief. In this intellectual framework belief in diabolical witchcraft was not a superstition, and opponents of this belief operating within the framework could not oppose it as such. It was part of a coherent, dominant world view. Only when a different world view evolved did the sceptics find firm intellectual ground on which to stand and dismiss witchcraft as superstitious.

The modern, liberal, sceptical historians of witchcraft failed to explain the decline of witchcraft because they insisted on seeing the controversy as a battle between superstition and reason and so were astonished that great and learned minds could have believed in witchcraft. They failed to realize that witchcraft was not a superstition before the new world view emerged in the mid-seventeenth century, and that all world views, including scientism, breed their own superstitions. Witchcraft declined because a new world view made it a superstition. It declined because it was as intellectually disreputable to defend witchcraft under the new system as it had been to attack it under the old.

The new world view was a philosophical and religious revolution that changed the whole concept of the cosmos and how it worked. The philosophical revolution was led by Descartes (1596–1650), who dismissed the tradition of medieval philosophy and argued for the existence of universal, observable, mechanical, and describable laws of nature that rendered the operation of demons (and angels) unnecessary and illogical. Later, Hume's scepticism went even further, and later still, scientific positivism declared that only those phenomena demonstrable by scientific method can reasonably be said to exist. To most people today who are brought up under the assumptions of positivism, belief in witchcraft has indeed become a superstition.

The religious revolution followed the philosophical revolution. Cartesianism led to the assumption of an orderly universe whose regular operations, ordained by the Deity from the beginning, were unlikely to be disturbed by the intervention of spiritual powers. God would have no wish to upset the laws he himself had established; much less would he give the Devil power to do so. Mysterious events, whether supposed miracles caused by God or supposed *maleficia* brought about by the power of the Devil, were either false reports or could be assigned a material explanation. The 'liberal' religious thought that grew out of the Enlightenment abandoned the ancient struggle between the good Lord and the evil Devil, each of whom intervened

René Descartes. The replacement of Aristotelian by Cartesian thought during the seventeenth century helped bring about the end of witch beliefs, at least among the educated.

in the operations of nature, and postulated instead a dispassionate, just, orderly, rational Deity. Pietism and optimism reinforced the idea of a kindly and reasonable God, and the idea has remained to the present – for better or worse – among most of those who maintain belief in God at all. This bloodless God being superfluous in the mechanical view of the universe, the result of diluted Christianity has been increasing atheism. Liberal religion naturally perceived belief in witchcraft as a stupid superstition, since there was no logical role for it in the mechanical world. After about 1700, few people with any claim to intellectual respectability dared claim a belief in witchcraft. The clergy either modified their views to reflect the new ideas or found themselves unheard.

The difference was enormous. Whereas in the sixteenth century Montaigne's position of 'eternal doubt' was largely ignored, a century later the more advanced scepticism of Malebranche was almost universally accepted, at least among the élite. In 1674, Malebranche argued that witchcraft and demonic possession were a delusion produced by overactive imaginations and the use of soporific drugs. Those who imagine that they go out to sabbats or change their shapes are unable to distinguish between their dreams and physical reality. Jesus Christ has redeemed the world, and Satan no longer has power over those who are reborn in the Lord. Malebranche believed that God might rarely for special reasons give Satan limited power to work harm and that sorcerers might occasionally work charms and incantations, but that these things were very rare.

Malebranche's position was very moderate and transitional; others were going much further. Cyrano de Bergerac's 'Letter against Witches' (1654) ridiculed all belief in witchcraft as arrant nonsense and blamed it (mistakenly) on the ignorance and folly of the common people. In England, as we have seen, Francis Hutchinson's *Historical Essay* in 1718 was the last work of importance that found it necessary to attack witchcraft in a serious vein. Laughter and mockery were taking the place of serious argument, and ridicule kills a belief more quickly than the weightiest logic. It was not until the beginning of the nineteenth century that intellectuals again took witchcraft seriously, and it was in wholly different perspective. Goya's paintings, certainly the most terrifying representations of witchcraft ever made, saw that understanding witch beliefs required a deep psychological grasp of the state of mind of witch and witch-hunter.

The intellectual erosion of witchcraft was accompanied by institutional erosion. The frenzy of witch-hunting destroyed itself when even credulous judges began to perceive that things were out of control. Already in the mid-seventeenth century believing judges were simply finding it difficult to distinguish between the innocent and the guilty. They were troubled that numbers of innocent people were possibly being sent to the stake and appalled at the destruction of whole communities by the witch trials. Fear of witches, fear of being accused of witchcraft, and terror of torture were making life in many regions almost unbearable. A commission at Calw in Germany in 1683, noting the destruction wrought by the witch trials, raised the possibility that the trials were themselves the work of the Devil, who had induced the fear of witchcraft in the Christian community in order to turn it against itself and destroy it. In fact, the spread of the trials and the increasing promiscuity of the accusations led eventually to one of two conclusions: either the Devil was so increasing his power that the end of the world must be near, or else, if Christ still ruled, the witch prosecutions must be a delusion. Opinions varied, but both the change in the intellectual world view and the lurid excesses of the trials assured the victory of the second opinion.

Like Salem in America and Mora in Sweden, the Loudun incident did much in France to encourage scepticism. Judges, physicians, and theologians debated the Loudun case at length in the Paris of the 1630s and 1640s, and few were able to deny that it was in large part a fraud. The implication of priests in the shameful events at Loudun and Louviers also gave rise to trepidation on the part of the clergy and the professions in general. Accusations of witchcraft were not confined to the poor and ignorant; as they

Opposite: frontispiece to Francis Hutchinson's *Historical Essay* (second edition, 1720), the book that put an end to witch beliefs among the educated in England.

AN
HISTORICAL ESSAY
CONCERNING
WITCHCRAFT.
WITH
OBSERVATIONS
UPON
MATTERS OF FACT;

Tending to clear the Texts of the Sacred
Scriptures, and confute the vulgar Errors a-
bout that Point.

AND ALSO
TWO SERMONS:
One in Proof of the Christian Religion; the
other concerning Good and Evil Angels.

By FRANCIS HUTCHINSON, D.D. Chaplain
in Ordinary to His Majesty, and Minister of
St. *James*'s Parish in St. *Edmund's-Bury*.

PSALM xxxi. 6. *I have hated them that hold fu-
perstitious Vanities: but I trust in the Lord.*
1 TIM. iv. 7. *But refuse profane and old Wives Fa-
bles, and exercise thy self rather unto Godliness.*

The SECOND EDITION, with confiderable Additions.

LONDON:
Printed for R. KNAPLOCK, at the *Bishop's Head*, and
D. MIDWINTER, at the *Three Crowns*, in St. *Paul's*
Church-yard. MDCCXX.

touched the ruling élite more frequently, members of the élite began to fear for their own safety. By the end of the Thirty Years War witch-hunting began to encounter official government opposition in Germany. Punishment of casual and false accusers became more severe, and the complexion of the indictments changed. Charges of simple sorcery – divination, charms, magical treasure-hunting – remained common, but, as had been the case centuries earlier, these were no longer united with charges of diabolism. Poisoning and infanticide were increasingly viewed by the courts as murder by physical rather than by magical means. The concept of *maleficium* lost its vitality, and the theological superstructure of diabolism, weakened by intellectual changes, was ready to collapse when the substructure of *maleficium* was undermined.

Witch beliefs naturally lingered longest in conservative rural areas: witchcraft was begotten in the cities but laid to rest in the countryside. In England, after the statute of 1736 repealed the laws against witchcraft, villagers continued to use informal and illegal means of seeking redress against witches, including lynching. In Hertfordshire in 1751 an elderly couple suspected of witchcraft were attacked by a mob which ransacked the workhouse in which they were living, dragged them two miles to water, stripped them, and threw them in. When they rose to the surface, they were thrust down until they were choked, then dragged out and beaten to death. Such occasional atrocities occurred well into the twentieth century, but they were no longer condoned by society. The leader of the Hertfordshire mob was convicted and hanged as a murderer.

Other social changes helped undermine belief in witchcraft. If lack of charity or kindness to a neighbour were often at the root of witch accusations, change in society's response to poverty and need could alter the pattern. In England, the National Poor Law (1601, amended 1722, 1782, and 1785) converted the support of the poor into a legal obligation of the community, relieving the individual from feeling guilt about the poor (though it did not prevent the Hertfordshire crime). The movement of the seventeenth century towards a 'combination of a less collectivist religion, a market economy, greater social mobility, [and] growing separation of people through the formation of institutional rather than personal ties' weakened witch beliefs.[52] The chief effect of shifting social conditions on witchcraft remained indirect. Witch beliefs shrivelled and disappeared once their intellectual vitality had been sapped. A world view that insisted upon natural explanations of events meant that one was more likely to blame the death of a cow or the illness of a child on natural causes than upon sorcery and demons.

As witchcraft declined, different kinds of occult phenomena took its place. The Black Mass was never part of the history of witchcraft. It appeared for the first time during the reign of Louis XIV. In 1673 some priests informed the Paris police that penitents were confessing that they had used poison to resolve marital difficulties. On investigation, the police discovered an international ring of poisoners and vast stores of poison. The evidence persuaded the king to establish a secret court to investigate the matter. The court, established in 1679, was called the *Chambre ardente* because the room in which it sat was draped in black and lit with candles. Many distinguished

Opposite: Goya, *La Lampara del Diablo, c.* 1794–5. Goya satirized witch beliefs, illustrating their grotesque inhumanity and their roots in ignorance and terror.

Man consulting a witch. The witch draws a magic circle around her client in order to protect him from evil spirits during the spell, but this does not prevent the Devil from placing a fool's cap on his head. In the sceptical thought of the eighteenth century, one who consulted a magician was a fool. The picture combines the old hag of witchcraft with the magic circle and candles of high magic.

people were among those prosecuted, but severe sentences including execution were handed down exclusively to the poor and uninfluential. At first the charges were limited to the use of substances such as poisons, abortants, aphrodisiacs, and other drugs, but in 1680 a number of priests were accused of saying black masses on the bodies of naked girls and sexually abusing them; they allegedly performed ritual copulation, desecrated the sacraments, mixed loathsome substances in the chalice, and sacrificed children. Some of the charges may have been true, but they do not constitute real witchcraft or even real Satanism, but a perverted parody of Christian service, a grotesque refinement introduced by the fevered baroque brain. The charges touched the court and even the king's former mistress Madame de Montespan, who was accused of plotting to poison the king and his new mistress Mademoiselle de Fontanges. The king, judging that the investigations had got out of hand, ordered them stopped; in 1682 he issued an edict denying the reality of witchcraft and eliminating prosecutions for witchcraft and sorcery. The conservatism of the provinces, however, allowed isolated witch trials and executions to continue in France for another sixty years.

The case of Catherine Cordière at Aix-en-Provence in 1731 is another example of how witchcraft was being replaced by other dark phenomena of the soul. Jean-Baptiste Girard, a Jesuit priest, was accused of using sorcery to seduce Catherine, a beautiful girl of about twenty-one who was obsessed with the idea of becoming a saint. Catherine related her visions and mystical experiences to Father Girard, and the priest seems to have been convinced of her holiness and agreed to aid her in her devotions. Their relationship gradually became excessive and improper. Then, at some point, Father Girard dismissed Catherine's visions as false, and the resentful girl began to manifest convulsions, hallucinations, and other forms of hysteria. She accused the priest of using demonic aid to debauch her. Father Girard was arrested, but after a long trial the charges were dismissed. Witchcraft in the classical sense was virtually absent from the trial, and demonism gave way to explicit and lurid sexuality. In an increasingly secularized world sensations would continue to appear, but they would no longer be linked with demonism.

In such a secularized world where witchcraft beliefs were superstitions, revivals of demonic belief (except in some remote rural areas) were wholly artificial. In England in the eighteenth century, Sir Francis Dashwood presided over the Hellfire Club, which boasted a number of distinguished and liberated spirits, including Benjamin Franklin. The club met in natural caves in Buckinghamshire to enjoy food, drink, gaming, and sex. As in the old tradition, they met underground, at night, secretly, and practised something like orgies. But they did so in jesting parody. They enjoyed their reputations as rakehells, but none of them believed in either hell or the Devil, and their salutations to Satan were wholly jocular (of course the Devil's best wile is to persuade us that he does not exist, and the Church of Satan is likely to be materialistic, hedonistic, anti-spiritual, élitist, and cynical). In the late eighteenth and nineteenth centuries no educated person believed that witchcraft had ever existed or ever could exist and folk wisdom, always at least half a century behind the intellectuals, followed, proclaiming that 'there is no such thing as a witch'. Simple sorcery continued, and grimoires, popular 'do-it-yourself' books based in part on cabbalistic sources but more on the traditions of simple sorcery, began to be published in the eighteenth century and have remained popular in rural areas into the twentieth. But the diabolical witch returned to the realm of fantasy whence she had sprung.

THE ROMANTIC REVIVAL

Even as folk wisdom turned at last against belief in witchcraft, however, the hint of a new point of view among the intellectuals was already appearing at the beginning of the nineteenth century. In 1828 Karl Ernst Jarcke argued that witchcraft was a nature religion that had continued through the Middle Ages into the present. It was the ancient religion of the German people,

which the Church had falsely condemned as Devil-worship. Such a position stemmed from a romanticism that glorified the past and a nationalism that glorified Germany. The tradition exemplified by Jarcke bore hideous fruit a century later when the Nazis proclaimed their pseudo-revival of the ancient religion of the Teutons. In 1829, the French writer Lamothe-Langon, who also fabricated an alleged collection of the private memoirs of Louis XVIII, published a number of documents relating to witchcraft in the fourteenth century which he claimed to have transcribed from records of the inquisition that had subsequently been destroyed. The effect of the fabrications was to establish what looked something like an organized witch-cult as early as the fourteenth century and thus to lend more credence to the idea that witchcraft might have been an old religion surviving through the Middle Ages.

Romanticism helped the revival of the idea of witchcraft in England as well as in Germany. In 1830 Sir Walter Scott published his *Letters on Demonology and Witchcraft*, which, owing to Scott's popularity and prestige, had a great effect in reviving interest in witchcraft. None of these new writers argued that witchcraft was a diabolical cult or that the witch trials should be reinstated. Quite the contrary, they believed that the alleged witches had been misunderstood and mistreated. But they did take a position markedly different from the rationalists of the eighteenth century who denied that witchcraft had existed at all. In 1839 Franz-Josef Mone argued that witchcraft derived from a pre-Christian clandestine cult of the Graeco-Roman world, a cult connected with Dionysos and Hecate and practised in the lower strata of society. Mone's argument had an impact upon a world frightened of revolutionary excesses and afraid of secret societies. In 1862, Jules Michelet took Mone's argument and stood it on its head. Witchcraft did originate in the lowest social levels, Michelet argued, but this was admirable: witchcraft was an early manifestation of the democratic spirit. It arose among the oppressed peasants of the Middle Ages, who adopted the remnants of an ancient fertility cult in protest against the oppression of Church and feudal aristocracy. Michelet's argument that witchcraft was a form of protest was adapted later by the Marxists; his argument that it was based on a fertility cult was adopted by anthropologists at the turn of the century, influencing Sir James Frazer's *Golden Bough*, Jessie Weston's *From Ritual to Romance*, Margaret Murray's *Witch-Cult in Western Europe*, and indirectly T.S. Eliot's *The Waste Land*.

Interest in the occult grew in the jaded world of the late nineteenth century. The Rosicrucians and the Order of the Temple of the Orient (O.T.O.) – secret, semi-élite magical societies – were gaining reputations. In France, the abbé Boullan, Eliphas Lévi, and J.K. Huysmans prompted the revival. In England, where spiritualism had long been prominent, occult movements proliferated. Of these the most influential was the Hermetic Order of the Golden Dawn, which boasted as members noted writers such as William Butler Yeats, Algernon Blackwood, Arthur Machen, Bram Stoker, and Sir Edward Bulwer-Lytton as well as dedicated occultists such as MacGregor Mathers, A.E. Waite, and Aleister Crowley, who styled himself The Great Beast. The Hermetic Order of the Golden Dawn delighted in literary and occult jokes and impostures. Crowley and Mathers

Opposite: Sir Francis Dashwood worshipping Venus. This satirical engraving after a painting by Hogarth shows the founder of the Hellfire Club at the mouth of his cave, where, dressed as a friar, he worships his gods: sex, food, and drink.

Eliphas Lévi, *The Sabbatic Goat*, 1896. One of the leaders of modern occultism, Lévi gave magical beliefs a new and pseudo-scientific basis. His portrait of Satan draws upon traditional iconography and adds modern occult symbolism, notably the androgynous characteristics.

Opposite: Aleister Crowley, *Self-portrait*, a dramatized drawing of the master with a phallic symbol on his head and a medallion round his neck with the inscription 'The Great Beast 666', a reference to the Book of Revelation.

engaged in a lurid feud in which they sent out spiritual powers against one another: Mathers sent a vampire to attack Crowley, and Crowley responded by sending Beelzebub and forty-nine subordinate demons to assault Mathers. Crowley wore a special perfume made of ambergris, musk, and civet, which he claimed made him irresistible to women. The Hermetic Order of the Golden Dawn translated cabbalistic books and grimoires and devised creative systems of numerology, spells, curses, and aphrodisiacs of its own.

DO WHAT THOU WILT

TO MEGA
THERION
666

Above left: Leila Waddell, one of Aleister Crowley's women, *c.* 1912. Crowley liked to mark his numerous lovers with what he called 'the sign of the beast'.

Above right: MacGregor Mathers (1854–1918), one of Crowley's chief rivals for leadership among occultists, performing rites of Isis that he had invented.

The elements of ceremonial magic that presently appear in modern witchcraft can be traced back to the influence of Crowley upon Gerald Gardner, the founder of modern witchcraft, and Crowley's own devotion, half-serious though it was, to Pan also helped develop Gardner's neopaganism. Crowley's *Hymn to Pan* is too violent for most neopagans, but it has a glorious vigour of its own. It concludes:

> With hoofs of steel I race on the rocks
> Through solstice stubborn to equinox.
> And I rave; and I rape and I rip and I rend
> Everlasting, world without end,
> Mannikin, maiden, maenad, man,
> In the might of Pan.

The great god Pan, who, according to legend, had died when Christ was born, seems not to have perished after all. In the last few decades he and his fellow gods and goddesses have enjoyed a small but growing revival. With the end of the witch-craze, diabolical witchcraft virtually disappeared, but a new kind of witchcraft, based on the worship of the old gods, has appeared.

Pan teaching the infant
Olympus to play the pipes.
The Greek god of the wild,
Pan provided many of the
iconographic characteristics of
the Devil, and modern
occultists chose him as a
symbol of opposition to
Christ and Christianity.

Alex Sanders, leader of the
'Alexandrians', an important
element of modern witchcraft in
England and America, dressed in
his robes of office.

8 Survivals and revivals

On 23 June 1978 a metropolitan newspaper reported a formal wedding in an article entitled 'Bewitching Wedding':

Between 70 and 80 witches and guests attended the ceremony that united the couple in the traditional Wiccan handfast. As the ceremony began . . . barefooted witches wearing robes of all colours and guests formed an arch of lighted white tapers leading from the house to the circle where the ceremony took place. . . . The couple was led in front of an altar draped in red velvet, and adorned on each side by candelabra. Witches and guests, still holding lighted tapers, were also anointed and, because of the large number attending, formed two circles, symbolizing no beginning or end. The couple dressed in long white robes with garlands of daisies, myrtle, and laurel on their heads . . .[53]

Reports of witches' weddings and witches' sabbats appear more and more frequently in newspapers, on television, and in popular books. A number of new journals and magazines are dedicated wholly or in part to witchcraft. Several thousand witches are active in Britain, perhaps ten thousand in North America, and more around the world. Witches have been murdered in Germany. Cinema and television have produced a turgid flow of lurid portraits of witchcraft. Advertisements appear in newspapers and magazines offering to divulge the secrets of witchcraft and to train new witches (for a fee).

The rationalists of the eighteenth century would have been surprised and doubtless dismayed to learn that the witch beliefs they had struggled to destroy were surviving – and reviving – two centuries later. But what *survived* is quite different from what *revived*. Survivals include simple sorcery, which persists the world over, and the combination of sorcery and Christian heresy known as Satanism or diabolism. Revivals include ceremonial magic (such as that of the Hermetic Order of the Golden Dawn), and the resurrection of ancient paganism. Sorcery, Satanism, and ceremonial magic are peripheral to this book and are treated briefly; our chief concern will be with the increasingly visible and significant neopagan revival.

MODERN SORCERY

Opposite: a wedding invitation from two modern neopagans. Isaac Bonewits holds a Bachelor's Degree in Magic from the University of California; he is the author of *Real Magic* (1971).

Sorcery, often tinged with diabolism, is still found all over Europe, particularly among peasants, although a rapid decline in such beliefs has occurred since the Second World War. Its characteristics vary according to region. German, French, English, Celtic, Italian, and Slavic sorcery each has its own distinguishing features. In Germany sorcery has recently become notorious again.

Deborah
Selene
Maenka
Kumin

and

Philip
Emmons
Isaac
Bonewits

are having
a wedding / celebration / circus

Bring instruments

on Sunday, August 6, 1978
3 p.m. ☉ Leo ☽ Virgo

at Redwood Bowl
(map on back)

Potluck feast and party to follow

Wear your favorite clothing

Gifts are totally optional   Let us know if you're coming

The sociologist Hans Sebald reports that in a German village in 1976 a poor, elderly, and isolated spinster named Elisabeth Hahn was suspected of being a witch and of keeping three familiars in the form of dogs.

The villagers shunned her, children threw rocks at her, and a hostile neighbor threatened to beat her to death because of hexes he felt she cast on him. One day, this neighbor set fire to her house, killing most of her animals, badly burning her, and totally destroying her home.[54]

In another German village that same year a young girl named Anneliese Michel died as a result of a long and strenuous exorcism performed by two priests of the diocese. Even more lurid was the case of Bernadette Hasler in 1969. Bernadette was a young girl whose parents fell under the influence of a vicious ex-priest and his mistress. Under their power, the girl confessed to worshipping Satan and to having 'married him'; he appeared to her almost nightly as a large man wearing black fur and slept with her. Having elicited this confession, the sadistic cultists endeavoured literally to beat the evil spirit out of the girl, who died next day as a result of their ministrations.

An elderly German scholar, Johann Kruse of Hamburg, has devoted most of his life to combating such beliefs, and he has collected a vast treasury of books, articles, letters, pictures, and other materials on German witchcraft, a collection now housed in the Hamburg Museum of Folklore. The personal letters are the most extraordinary. Many come from people who claim to have lived closely for years with a secret witch. Hating and fearing this witch, who may be spouse, landlord, or neighbour, they turn to Kruse for help. Most suspected witches are women, and frequently one woman will accuse another woman who is competing with her for the affections of a man. The motive of sexual jealousy may go a long way towards explaining the preponderance of women among those accused, since the majority of accusers also are women; the professional witch-hunters, the *Hexenbanner*, however, are almost always men.

The effects of witch belief go far beyond mere suspicion. A woman suspected of witchcraft in 1952 wrote Kruse a frightened letter describing how an elderly couple were driven out of their son's home because their daughter-in-law had fetched the *Hexenbanner* in a car and demonstrated to her husband that his parents were witches. Sometimes the writer is so terrified and upset as to be uncertain whether he has been bewitched or whether he has magical powers himself. One letter dated 1974 is a plea for help from a woman who believed herself to have suffered harm from a witch as a child, had later become a member of a religious group that she later fled after discovering they used black magic, and then had suffered for years from the evil spells of her mother-in-law, who among other things had bought and used teddy bears representing her son, her daughter-in-law, her granddaughter, and her daughter-in-law's mother. These fears, though they appear to be silly, were no joke to the woman: her letter shows that she is terrified. It concludes:

By chance I acquired a copy of the Sixth and Seventh Books of Moses [grimoires]. They contain a few things that I can use to protect myself, but they have not helped much. I am afraid that they [the witches] will destroy us all? Is there no help?

Kruse opposes all belief in witchcraft and has attempted to end the publication and dissemination of the popular grimoires entitled the 'Sixth and Seventh Books of Moses'. Allegedly lost books of the Bible, these magical handbooks contain a mélange of medieval ideas and modern folk tradition. Written no earlier than the eighteenth century, they still have enormous influence among the semi-literate: a new edition appeared as recently as 1977. Most of all Kruse dislikes the *Hexenbanner*, the cunning folk who sell remedies and counter-magics. Born in 1889, Kruse at the age of twelve experienced witchcraft in his own village. A farmer with sick cattle summoned the *Hexenbanner*, who fumigated the barn with *Teufelsdreck* (asafoetida) and told the farmer that whatever person came first to his farm the next day would be the witch who was hexing his cattle. Early next morning an old woman arrived and was immediately accused as a witch. Kruse estimates that at present thousands of *Hexenbanner* continue to be active, sometimes harming or killing people with their remedies, sometimes inciting hatred and violence against the supposed witches.

The usual course of events is like this: a child or a farm animal becomes ill. The family cannot find a physical cause. They consult the *Hexenbanner* directly or are referred to a *Hexenbanner* by a friend or by a fortune-teller. The *Hexenbanner* is probably someone in their own village, but sometimes the 'victims' will seek out one who by reason of his fame is in great demand and travels from place to place earning not inconsiderable sums. One well-known *Hexenbanner* named Eberling specialized in divination with bedfeathers to diagnose the hex. *Hexenbanner* use a variety of herbs, some, like the asafoetida, useful in exorcising because of their powerful fumigating properties, others, folk medicine containing real or imagined curative drugs. Psychological investigations of the *Hexenbanner* reveal that their primary motivation is not venality. Of Eberling the investigators reported that he was fanatically convinced of his own mission and believed the laws against such practices to be unfair and harmful. Arrested, he compared his arraignment and trial with that of Jesus Christ.

Hans Sebald has written a thorough and perceptive study of witchcraft in modern Germany. Anyone, Sebald says, is supposed to be able to work witchcraft with access to information such as that contained in the alleged Books of Moses. But some people were identified as witches, usually those who were thought to cast spells habitually, who acted malevolently, or who had unpleasant dispositions. General belief is that such malevolent magic is done with the help of the Devil or demons. Sebald observes ironically that the peasants talk much about the danger that witchcraft poses to their immortal souls, but they almost always lodge accusations relating to physical damage to health, animals, or property. Women are accused of witchcraft approximately ten times more often than men. Sebald reports a typical accusation:

One afternoon, a peasant boy surprised a number of unfamiliar chickens in the barn, stealing grain from the freshly threshed crop. The ruckus resulting from the boy's chasing the birds from the premises brought the neighbor woman, the owner of the chickens, to the scene. She was irate and threatened: 'You just wait, you'll pay for this!' When the boy woke up the next morning, he found his body teeming with lice, while his brother with whom he shared the bed was not bothered with one. The agonizing visitation continued in this most exclusive manner for several weeks until, no longer able to stand the discomfort, the boy went for advice to the village shepherd. The man nodded knowingly and suggested that the boy go to the angry neighbor and beg for forgiveness. Without hesitation, the boy followed the advice and the lice vanished as suddenly as they had appeared.[55]

Such occurrences, common in the 1930s and even the 1950s, are rarer today, partly as a result of work such as that of Johann Kruse, and partly as a result of the triumph of the new mythologies spread by television. Sebald observes that now most children are unfamiliar with the old beliefs. But their elders still believe that witches do what they were supposed to do during the witch-craze: they cause nightmares, give the evil eye, raise storms, bring about accidents and diseases, and harm crops, homes, and animals. They dry up a milch cow or steal its milk: an effective way of doing this without attracting attention is to stay at home and milk the corners of a tablecloth or other fabric: this will bring the milk out of your neighbour's cows into your own home. Witches use secret books and keep familiars such as black cats and dogs. They are particularly dangerous to children. They ride through the air at night and attend orgies. And they make pacts with the Devil, who takes their allegiance and their souls in exchange for the magical powers he gives them. This is the historical synthesis of sorcery and diabolism that was the basis of the witch-craze, and if the long tradition is now coming to an end it is no pity.

SATANISM

Pact with the Devil, so central to the historical tradition, forms the basis of one modern revival: Satanism. Satanism today is quite different from historical witchcraft, however, and it is totally rejected by all the neopagan witches today. Modern witches observe that since they reject Christianity they can scarcely be supposed to worship the Christian Devil. I describe Satanism here only so that the lack of resemblance between it and witchcraft may be clear.

Most modern Satanists do not believe in Satan or the Devil in any real sense. Those who really worship the personification of evil are extremely rare. Some claim to worship 'Lucifer', whom they suppose to be an ancient deity which Christians mistakenly or maliciously identified with the Devil. But for the most part Satanists are mere hedonists, combining devotion to sensual pleasure with theatrical occult thrills. Of these the most prominent is Anton Szandor LaVey, whose 'church of Satan', established in 1966 and found in the San Francisco telephone directory under 'Churches: Satanist', has contrived to attract a great deal of international publicity.

LaVey, a former lion-tamer, calliopist, palm-reader, and police photographer, uses his show-biz background to the utmost in his dramatically decorated house, his use of swords, candles, incense, incantations, and, of course, nude women on the altar. Arguing that Satan is not the opponent of God but rather a 'hidden force in nature', LaVey insists that the power of magic is not without but within, in the control of our

Anton Szandor LaVey. Self-styled high priest of Satanism, LaVey runs the
'First Church of Satan' in San Francisco. Modern witches vehemently reject any
connection with Satanism and consider LaVey a charlatan.

psychological forces. The purpose of Satanism is to acquire and to control, and one does this by openly admitting and accepting one's passions. The seven cardinal sins of Christianity are to be encouraged since in accepting and working with them we can accomplish our desires. Anger, lust, greed, and pride are virtues. 'Satanism is a blatantly selfish, brutal philosophy. It is based on the belief that human beings are inherently selfish, violent creatures.' These are not the words of LaVey's opponents but of the introduction to LaVey's popular manifesto, *The Satanic Bible*.[56] LaVey, determinedly materialistic, rejects contemporary witchcraft as namby-pamby ethicalism and dismisses ceremonial magic as 'sanctimonious fraud' and 'esoteric gibberish'.[57] The contemptible Judaeo-Christian religion is the root of our present misery, for it has taught us to repress our true, selfish feelings. Eastern religions are not much better. On the whole, LaVey's *Bible* is crude popular psychology seasoned with black altars, gongs, bells, chalices, and nudity. Why bother with such trappings? Because, LaVey explains, 'man needs ceremony and ritual, fantasy and enchantment, [the] wonder and fantasy which religion, in the past, has provided.'[58]

LaVey's own disbelief in magic is patent:

The definition of magic, as used in [*The Satanic Bible*] is: The change in situations or events in accordance with one's will, which would, using normally accepted methods, be unchangeable. This admittedly leaves a large area for personal interpretation.[59]

One can become a high priest or priestess and command one of LaVey's 'grottoes' if one has enough money and influence.

LaVey has an exaggerated view of his own importance:

People, organizations, nations are making millions of dollars off us. What would they do without us? Without the Church of Satan, they wouldn't have anybody to rage at and to take the blame for all the rotten things happening in the world.[60]

Little connects LaVey's Satanism with either traditional European witchcraft or with modern neopagan witchcraft. The most notable, and the most evil, aspect of LaVey's cult is its trivialization of evil. By trumpeting the virtues of 'evil' in terms of personal greed and lust, LaVey ignores those who have had to suffer the real evils of napalm, rape, extermination camps, and mutilations.

Much closer to gross reality – and to real Satanism – is the cult of Charles Manson. No hypocritical game with candles and chalices, Manson's religion is a true creed of torture and death, presided over by a man who called himself 'the Devil, Satan'.[61] At the time of the multiple murders at Sharon Tate's house in 1969, Charlie's follower Tex announced: 'I am the Devil and I'm here to do the Devil's business.'[62] The virtually illiterate Manson derived his ideas from movies, magazines, and talk. In some mystical fashion, he seems to believe that Satan and Christ, good and evil, were to be unified, perhaps in the person of Charlie himself. But Manson has no more to do with witchcraft than with the Presbyterian Church. Popular accounts linking the Manson Family with witchcraft are simply ignorant. Modern witches do not worship, or even believe in, the principle of evil.

Opposite: Charles Manson. Manson is much more a real Satanist than LaVey. Lurid accounts in the American media incorrectly linked Manson with witchcraft. There is no connection between modern, neopagan witchcraft, and the Manson cult.

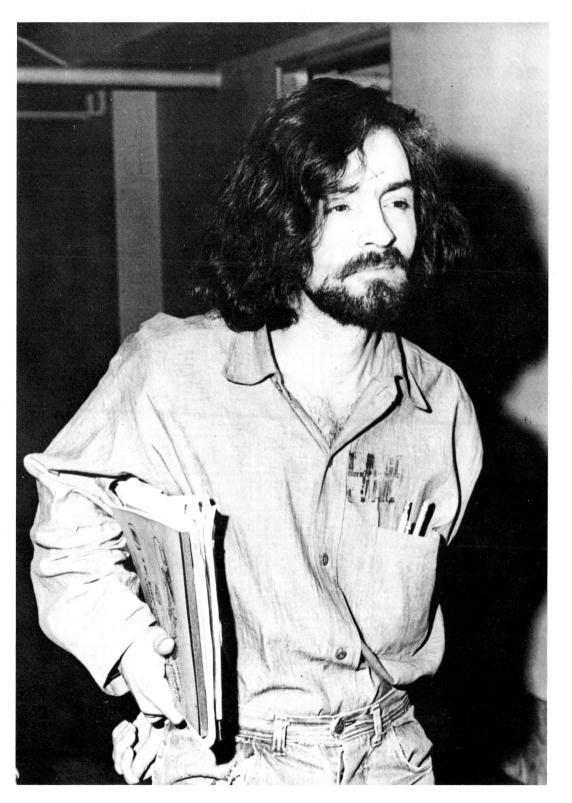

9 The religion of the witches

The religion of modern witchcraft is a revival of paganism. But not all modern witches are neopagans. Some, such as Sybil Leek, are family traditionalists, following ideas believed to have been passed down through their families for generations. Some are psychic, 'natural' witches. Most witches believe that everyone has some psychic powers but that some are more gifted than others. Such people are often called 'witches' by others and then decide to adopt the name for themselves. Such witches often claim to be hereditary, 'genetic' witches. Some draw upon the Cabbala, Sufism, or Eastern religions. Some are feminists whose beliefs and practices are a variety of neopaganism. Possibly 15 per cent of modern witches – more in America than in England – are neopagan feminists.

THE RISE OF NEOPAGAN WITCHCRAFT

Neopagan witchcraft has roots in the historical tradition of Michelet, who argued that European witchcraft was the survival of an ancient religion. This idea influenced Sir James Frazer and a number of other anthropologists and writers in the late nineteenth and early twentieth centuries. The publication of Charles Leland's *Aradia* in 1899 was an important step in the evolution of the new religion of witchcraft.

Charles Leland was a widely read and widely travelled American writer and folklorist who while staying in Italy in 1866 learned that a manuscript containing the ancient secrets of Italian witchcraft was in existence. He had been relying upon an Italian witch named Maddalena to find him folkloric materials, and Maddalena produced for his pleasure a manuscript entitled *Aradia, or the Gospel of the Witches*. Or she produced something like that. For Leland admitted that he never saw *Aradia* in 'an old manuscript', but rather had heard it orally from Maddalena and seen portions of it transcribed in her handwriting. The criticism of *Aradia* made by Elliot Rose in his *Razor for a Goat* (1962) is compelling, and I do not need to repeat his arguments here. The doctrines and practices of the witches as reported by Leland are a mélange of sorcery, medieval heresy, witch-craze concepts, and political radicalism, and Leland reports ingenuously that this is just what he expected, since it fitted what he had read in Michelet. (Some of the doctrines did surprise him, possibly a tribute to Maddalena's imperfect understanding of her patron's requirements.)

Aradia may simply have been faked by Leland, though his own explanatory appendix seems too frank for that. Or Maddalena may have been a fraud, though that is difficult to say as no documentation exists of

Sybil Leek, the best-known witch of modern England, does a bit of magic at a crossroads near her home in Hampshire.

what she did tell him. Leland never produced either Maddalena or her handwritten notes for the community of scholars. Perhaps the most likely interpretation is that Leland, already learned in folklore and fascinated by Michelet, enthusiastically read into Maddalena's words what he already knew – or thought he knew – about witchcraft. Clearly he imposed ideas gleaned from Michelet upon Maddalena's descriptions. He admits some of this in his own preface:

It is true that *I have drawn from other sources*, but this woman by long practice has perfectly learned what few understand, or *just what I want*, and how to extract it from those of her kind.[63]

Leland had asked Maddalena to teach him an invocation that would help him obtain ancient books and manuscripts cheaply, and perhaps in her

Aradia

or the

Gospel of the

Witches

by

Charles G. Leland.

London

David Nutt,

270-71 Strand,

1899

A drawing of a witch by Leland. Leland claimed to have found evidence that ancient traditions of worship of Diana had persisted into modern Italy.

eagerness to please she provided more than the charm. Anthropologists are familiar with the eager local who provides them with *just what they want*; more often than not it turns out to be the product of an enterprising local artisan. Leland, a political radical enchanted with Michelet's erroneous view that witches were socially oppressed rebels against feudalism, discovered in *Aradia*, to his great delight, passages reflecting radical views congenial with those of Michelet and of himself but incongruous with any tradition of witchcraft. Numerous explanations are conceivable. But *Aradia* is not what one would

Opposite: frontispiece to Charles Leland's *Aradia*, 1899, one of the sources of modern witchcraft.

expect of a surviving witch cult; it is very much what one would expect from a late-nineteenth-century scholar attempting (for whatever motive) to discover such a cult. To say the best for it, *Aradia* is unreliable.

Yet its ideas had great influence. *Aradia* speaks of the old religion, the *vecchia religione*, whose chief deity is Diana. Diana is created before all other beings and contains all things in herself. She divides herself into the light and the darkness – a myth deriving through Catharism from Mazdaism, not from any pagan (certainly not Roman) belief. The darkness she retains in herself, but the light she makes into Lucifer, her brother and her son. The unusual association of Lucifer with light rather than darkness derives from the original meaning of his name, 'Light-bearer', but he is no benevolent fertility god in *Aradia*, but a diabolical figure who is the most evil of all spirits reigning in hell. Attracted to the light, Diana changes herself into a cat and in that form makes love with her brother and son. The daughter of this union, Aradia or Herodias, is a goddess who acts as special patroness of Diana's worshippers, who are called 'witches', *strege*. Aradia was the first witch, *la prima strega*.

It is likely that Leland's work would never have had wide influence had it not been for the corroboration allegedly brought to it by Margaret Murray. As we saw in Chapter 2, the Murray thesis is that European witchcraft was a remnant of an ancient fertility religion based on the worship of the horned god Dianus. This old religion persisted through the Roman Empire, the Middle Ages, and on into the early modern period. Only at the end of the Middle Ages was Christianity powerful enough to launch an effective attack, and finally to wipe out the old religion during the persecutions of the witch-craze.

This scenario, like that of *Aradia*, is not permitted by the evidence, which Murray misused in violation of the simplest rules of criticism. All historians are agreed on this (see pp. 41–2). But most recent historians have taken the unwarranted position that it contains no truth at all. Open-minded investigation readily reveals that some – indeed many – pagan beliefs and practices survived through the Middle Ages into the present. The question is not *whether* survivals existed, but how many and of what kind.

Murray's ideas had intellectual vogue for a long while, but they did not immediately generate the witch revival. The religion of the witches came into being in the years immediately following the Second World War. In 1948, Robert Graves published *The White Goddess*, a brilliant, provocative, and uncritical tome in which he argued for the existence of a widespread and beautiful ancient cult, a cult not of the horned god but of the earth and moon goddess. Graves found this cult all over ancient Europe, especially in Celtic culture. At the same time, E. O. James was keeping interest in ancient survivals alive with a series of books on ancient religious rites and festivals.

At this juncture, witchcraft was becoming a reality in the mind of Gerald Gardner. Gardner was born in 1884. His followers tell the story that he was initiated into witchcraft in 1939 by Old Dorothy Clutterbuck, a witch of the New Forest who later, they say, led the covens of England to the seashore where they prevented Hitler's invasion by sending out the cone of power towards him with the instruction, 'You cannot come.' When the Craft was

destroyed in the 'Burning Time', it was argued, a few kept it alive secretly, and old Dorothy was the heir of this ancient tradition. In fact there is no evidence that old Dorothy ever existed, and the ancient tradition is very dubious. Aidan Kelly, a Berkeley scholar, has examined Gardner's papers and after long critical scrutiny is prepared to demonstrate that Gardner's ideas can be traced to other, modern sources. Kelly's reconstruction of Gardner's 'reform' of witchcraft is more or less as follows.

Gardner used a variety of literary and magical sources to invent – or re-invent – a religion. He had belonged to a number of magical and spiritualist organizations, including the Fellowship of Crotona, of which Annie Besant was also a member, and the Hermetic Order of the Golden Dawn. He was a friend of Aleister Crowley and claimed to have a charter from Crowley to found a chapter of the O.T.O. The influence of Crowley upon Gardner was considerable, and, drawing heavily from the Golden Dawn material, Gardner began to write a grimoire in his own handwriting. Gradually new ideas – ideas later to be the teachings, laws, and rituals of the Craft – worked their way into the material. This grimoire, still in existence in the Ripley's collection at Toronto, was begun during the Second World War. It is clear from this manuscript that, if Gardner had been initiated into a coven in 1939, they had given him almost no information at all. His ideas of the Craft were still very inchoate. The material gradually changed as Gardner's own views shifted from the élite ceremonial magic of the Golden Dawn to a more populist magic, transforming the semi-serious intellectual rituals of the Order into simpler rituals that could be performed by ordinary people. Gradually he reduced or eliminated the Judaeo-Christian-gnostic flavour of the Golden Dawn materials and added neopagan ideas derived from Murray and Leland. Later still, he absorbed ideas from Graves, James, and other writers. (Some scholars find the influence of Crowley even in Gardner's revised views

Gerald Gardner, the most important creator of modern witchcraft, standing in front of a witchcraft exhibit at his museum on the Isle of Man (now in Toronto).

and claim that Crowley, rather than Gardner, is the true father of modern witchcraft.)

At first Gardner's revision followed Murray closely and emphasized the importance of the horned god. But gradually the Goddess became more and more important, until she emerged as the chief deity. As the power of the Goddess rose, so did that assigned to the High Priestess, who replaced the High Priest as leader of the coven. By 'drawing down the moon', a High Priestess can take the Goddess's power into herself and, for a time, in effect become the Goddess. Gardner's combination of ceremonial magic with simple sorcery produced a new way of working magic appropriate to smaller and simpler groups. A good example of the development of Gardner's thought is the 161 laws of the Craft (which were first published in the appendix of June Johns' laudatory biography of Alex Sanders – for whom, see below). These laws purport to be from a Book of Shadows dating from the sixteenth century. In fact Kelly has proved that the first version of them was drafted by one of Gardner's associates and then rewritten in pseudo-archaic language by Gardner, supplemented with other material, and issued in 1958–9. The language is strained in itself, but the certain proof of its modernity is that in Gardner's manuscripts the modern-language versions of most of the passages in these 'laws' were composed *earlier* than the archaic version.

That Gardner (or Crowley) invented the religion does not invalidate it. Every religion has a founder, and much that surrounds the origin of every religion is historically suspect. Lack of historicity does not necessarily deprive a religion of its insight. But no religion based upon evidence that is *demonstrably* false is likely to survive long. That is why sophisticated witches have increasingly abandoned the argument that the Craft is an ancient religion based on a surviving tradition and argue instead for its validity in terms of its poetic, spiritual, and psychological creativity.

Gardner's books, especially his *Witchcraft Today*, are the foundation of modern witchcraft, and Gardnerians continue to flourish. Two types of Gardnerianism exist: (1) those groups claiming direct apostolic succession from Gardner's original coven, and (2) those who profess different origins but whose ideas are clearly derivative from Gardner. The leading example of the latter is Alex Sanders and his followers the Alexandrians. According to his followers, Sanders, who was born in 1926, was as a child initiated into witchcraft by his grandmother. Having great powers of precognition, Sanders saw the Battle of Britain in a crystal ball five years before it occurred. Led astray by greed and lust, and carried away by his own powers, Sanders turned to black magic, calling up demons and worshipping the Devil. At a time of personal crisis, when his sister was ill and near death, Sanders repented and turned his magic to good ends. Among other good deeds, he saved a child from a Catholic priest who was about to offer it up as a ritual sacrifice. We may be forgiven if we do not take all of this very seriously: for instance, stories of initiations by grandmothers are a common joke in the Craft. Sanders' doctrines and practices are for the most part derived from Gardner's.

A bewildering variety of other neopagan groups flourish in Britain and America. Having no common body of doctrine or common source or pattern

of authority, witches have few organizations transcending the local coven. A number have been established, but few have endured more than a year or two. Some of the recent organizations are the Pagan Front, the Pagan Movement, the Witchcraft Research Association, the Covenant of the Goddess, the Midwest Pagan Council, and the Association of Cymmry Wicca. These organizations are by and large tolerant, flexible, and undogmatic. The attractive emphasis on individual creativity and freedom presents a sociological problem. Witchcraft has so far not been effective in pressing its views in public: it has yet to gain theological or political credibility. So long as witches remain unorganized, they will continue to be ineffective. Yet if they do organize and establish doctrine and authority – if they 'transform sacrament into corporation' – their appealing freedom and creativity will be compromised.

Alex Sanders leading a ritual dance at the sabbat, which is often performed 'skyclad' – naked – in order to reduce inhibitions that might impede the flow of magical power.

WITCHCRAFT AND THE FEMINIST MOVEMENT

The pre-eminence of the Goddess in Gardnerian *thealogy* has made it attractive to some feminists. In 1968, WITCH, the Women's International

Bobbie, a California witch, at the outdoor altar of her coven.

Terrorist Conspiracy from Hell, was founded as a political protest group that took the name only in jest. A few of the WITCHes were surprised and intrigued to learn that there really were actual witches worshipping a female deity, and some went on to join the Craft. Feminism is a wide and diverse movement whose main thrust is political. But within feminism a cultural movement exists, and within the cultural movement a spiritual movement, and within the spiritual movement, the feminist Craft. Witches are at present only a small part of the feminist movement, and an uneasy tension exists between the movement and the Craft. Most feminists regard witchcraft (and indeed spirituality in general) as a foolish diversion from political goals. Many witches on the other hand resent the politicization of the Craft by feminist witches. But feminist witchcraft is at present the most rapidly growing segment of the Craft, and it is closely related to some broader *thealogical* movements. The radical theologian Mary Daly, for example, who moved steadily leftwards out of Catholicism, has expressed great sympathy for the religion of the Goddess; another indication of growing Christian interest in the goddess-principle is Andrew Greeley's book on the female nature of God (*The Mary Myth: on the Femininity of God*, 1977).

Feminist witches call themselves Dianic. Some Dianic covens are moderate, including men as well as women. Some exclude men: of these some covens are explicitly lesbian, while others are of mixed sexual preference. Feminist witches share a rejection of patriarchal religion, particularly of the Judaeo-Christian God, but also including the horned god of the Murray thesis. Some feminist covens accord the horned god secondary status to the Goddess, but most worship only the Goddess. Feminist witches tend to resent hierarchy in general and are more egalitarian than are covens with men in them.

A sense of feminist witchcraft may be obtained from the following quotations:

Where does energy come from? We know that supportive, creative energy exists in women, and we want to come together to share this. The same energy exists in nature, and we want to be closer to nature to share this force.[64]

Or this portion of a poem by Candice Haddad Campbell, 'Evocation of the Goddess':

> architect of the cell's alphabet
> navigator of blood's latitudes
> keeper of the archives of fire
>
> my heritage unwinds inside me
> uncoils like a long galaxy
> through the dark nucleoplasm
>
> like a snake gone opaque
> she hides in the jungles of the chromosome
>
> she lies at the hydrocarbon's heart
> she is the black hole itself
> between her thighs
> the universe is squeezed from spirit[65]

That the Goddess, so long suppressed by the masculine-orientated religions of the West, Judaism, Christianity, and Islam, should eventually re-emerge is perhaps inevitable.

WITCHCRAFT TODAY

The wide variety of witchcraft today makes all generalizations subject to more than the usual reservations. What follows is a schematic presentation of neopagan witchcraft. Statements such as 'witches do' or 'witches believe' must be read as 'some witches do' or 'many witches believe'.

Modern witchcraft is a variety of paganism. Most witches worship pagan deities – the gods and goddesses of the ancient Celts, Teutons, Greeks, or Egyptians. But not all pagans are witches. A witch is a pagan who, in addition to worshipping the gods, practises one or another variety of magic. A number of neopagan organizations exist with ties to the Craft but independent of it. Neopagans usually call their congregations 'groves' rather than covens and usually do not work magic. Witches sometimes use the term 'grove' for their outer court, which is open to all, but 'coven' for the inner court, which is closed to those who have not been initiated. The word 'coven', from the French *couvent* and the Latin *conventus*, means 'gathering' or 'meeting'. The coven appears first in the sixteenth century as a Scottish invention. Margaret Murray's intense interest in covens was transferred to Gardner, who made the coven the centre of modern witchcraft. The traditional number in a coven is thirteen, historically a parody of Christ and his apostles, though modern witches seek more ancient and congenial explanations. Some argue that thirteen is the greatest number that can workably fit into the nine-foot magic circle, others that in groups of more than thirteen a sense of working community is lost, so that the cone of power cannot be raised. Sometimes, when a number of covens meet together, as at a major festival, the circle is drawn larger, and some argue that the magic is then more powerful.

The most universal characteristic of witches is their love and veneration of nature, though some, surprisingly, dissent and glorify human power and mastery over nature. For most witches, the Deity is immanent in nature. Some witchcraft is a variety of pantheism. Perceiving the earth as a manifestation of the Goddess, the witches love and worship it, in contrast to the Judaeo-Christian tradition that makes humanity the exploiter of the world and sets men and women against nature. This latter tradition, having been transformed into its secularized twin, belief in material 'progress', has produced hideous factories, urban blight, exploitation of the poor, and spiritual dullness. The witches argue that a return to a closer identification of humanity with nature will be better both for the earth and for our own spirits. Thus the rites and festivals of witchcraft are attuned to the seasons, phases of the moon, and the other natural rhythms of the cosmos.

One modern witch, Tony Kelly, explains this point of view:

We will write the old myths as they were always written, and we will read them on the rocks and in the caves and in the deep of the greenwood's shade, and we will hear them in the rippling mountain streams and in the rustling of the leaves, and we will see them in the storm clouds, and in the evening mists. . . . There is magic in the heath far away from the cold grey society, and there are islands of magick hidden in the entrails of the metropoles behind closed doors, but the people are few and the barriers between us are formidable. The Old Religion has become a dark way, obscure and hidden in the protective bosom of the night. Thin fingers turn the pages of a Book of Shadows while the sunshine seeks in vain his worshippers in his leafy glades. . . . Man looked with one eye on a two-faced god when he reached for the heavens and scorned the Earth which alone is our life and our provider and the bosom to which we have ever returned since the dawn of time. He who looks only to reason to plumb the unfathomable is a fool.[66]

The chief deity of the witches is the Goddess, the deity of nature perceived as an earth Goddess, a moon Goddess, and a fertility Goddess. Witches emphasize the threefold nature of the Goddess: she is warrior maid; she is mother; she is hag of darkness and rebirth. The Goddess is called Isis, Astarte, Cerridwen, Ishtar, Anath, Kali, the Magna Mater, or any name that the witch feels responds to her own mythopoeic vision. Some feminist witches worship the Goddess as their sole deity; most worship both the Goddess and her consort, the horned god. Some introduce a seasonal consideration, worshipping the Goddess in the spring and summer (as Persephone she symbolizes the fertility of the earth in the time of growing) and shift at Hallowe'en to worshipping the God during the autumn and winter. The worship of the God and Goddess represents the principle of duality, the belief that the cosmos is divided into doublets: male and female, light and darkness, negative and positive. The sexual union of the God and Goddess represents the principle of unification. The hierogamy – the ritual union of priest and priestess – was practised in some ancient religions to draw down a powerful cosmic force, but this 'great rite' is seldom practised by modern witches.

The coincidence of the opposites symbolized by the union of male and female is a common principle in comparative religion, and it soundly addresses the Jungian principles of individuation and integration. In the Jungian process of individuation, the human mind begins in a state of indifferentiation: all is chaos, flux. Gradually the chaos is resolved into opposites, which struggle against one another. This state of tension is painful, and many people never resolve it. Some are able to bring the opposites together in harmonious union and thereby achieve full individuation. This process in the human soul is projected in mythology on to gods and cosmos. Mythologies and religions that address themselves to the union of opposites thus address themselves to a fundamental principle of growth in the human psyche. The union of God and Goddess in witchcraft is an ancient, powerful, and psychologically valid doctrine.

Some witches virtually ignore the other gods and goddesses; others are more actively polytheistic, worshipping the whole pantheon though giving the horned God and Goddess pride of place. Most witches take their deities seriously. For some they are metaphors of power inherent in the human unconscious, or metaphors of the powers of nature. For others, they are superhuman powers created by human belief in them. For yet others, they are eternal forces that are transcendent as well as immanent. Witches do believe in the gods, and many practise and feel this belief in an intensely personal way. Their variety of response as to what that belief means is not much greater than the variety of response among thoughtful Christians as to what belief in the Christian God means.

Virtually all witches firmly reject the Judaeo-Christian tradition. They have embraced the term 'pagan' and made it a term of honour. Yet their choice of the name poses a question. The Roman Christians were notoriously undiscriminating in their views of their opponents. They applied the term *pagan*, 'yokel', generously to Celtic, Syrian, and every other polytheist religion they encountered. Many of the pagans themselves accepted the validity of other cults for their worshippers, and 'it seems to have been a regular, if tacit, assumption in antiquity that all peoples worshipped about the same gods.'[67] Modern scholarship too perceives many similarities among pagan religions. But substantial differences also existed. Many modern witches appear to have a simplistic view that there was one ancient pagan religion. Others, more sophisticated, knowingly create a synthetic paganism of their own, combining diverse ancient traditions in what amounts to a new religion. Still others attach themselves to a modern version of a particular pagan religion such as Druidism. These distinctions are relatively unimportant in terms of what the witches are really driving at. The Goddess is an archetype of great and enduring power.

The figure of the horned god raises other questions. Horned fertility gods such as the Greek Pan or the Celtic Cernunnos are fairly common in religion, and it is reasonable that they should be prominent in neopaganism. But under the influence of Leland and Murray, some witches confuse this figure with that of Lucifer and claim that the Christians turned the horned god falsely into the lord of evil. This claim contains an element of truth, because the Christians drew heavily upon the attributes (horns, tail, hairy legs, hooves) of Pan and other deities for their pictures of the Devil. But the Devil's origins and development are totally separate from those of the horned god, and the name of Lucifer is simply a historical mistake. Further, the word 'Devil' means nothing like 'little god', as some witches claim.[68] The argument that the Christians during the witch-craze misunderstood or misrepresented the worship of the fertility god as the worship of the Devil is an illogical distortion of the evidence. What the Christians believed they were attacking was the principle of evil, the cosmic enemy. In the period 1300–1700 no one connected this figure with any ancient god (let alone Miss Murray's 'Dianus').

Whence then is evil? No religion or philosophy has found this easy to answer, including neopagan witchcraft. Like other polytheist/monist religions, witchcraft makes reference to the dark side of the Goddess without exploring how or why the divine principle is constructed in such a way that children are disfigured by napalm, prisoners disembowelled on meat hooks, or young men eaten away by cancer. When witches do try to explain evil, they sound very much like Christians: suffering teaches us and causes us to mature.

Comparative religion shows that ethics are not an essential component of religion. Yet most witches elect to be bound by a simple and benevolent moral code whose chief principle is 'Do what ye will an it harm none' ('Do whatever you like so long as it doesn't hurt anyone else'). Witches also enjoin a sense of responsibility for actions, including understanding that retribution will follow any evil action. Many subscribe to the threefold law: 'What good you do returns to you threefold; what harm you do also returns to you threefold.' One witch wrote to me:

We are *free* to live as the Goddess directs us. This is usually expressed as Fate but it is not Fate in the normally accepted fatalistic, pessimistic sense. However: *if* we violate this freedom, if we seek to thwart our Fate, then the Goddess exacts her own swift retribution *in this life*. She does not store it up for an after life or a reincarnated life. And she can be quite direct about it.[69]

Generally speaking, witches are quite charitable. One High Priest cautions against using magic to retaliate against one who has harmed you. Rather, he says, use positive magic to help the person adopt a happier and more constructive attitude towards you. Witchcraft generally aims at making a person psychologically more secure and happy. Witches stress the element of joy in their religion and compare their freedom from irrational guilt favourably with the ethics of Judaism and Christianity as typically taught. Witches generally agree with the philosophy of Epicurus: achieve satisfaction and joy by avoiding extremes and keeping balance. Many witches know how to use techniques of meditation and psychology in order to achieve this balance. The joyful person who is in control of his or her life, they argue, is best able to affect the world around him. The magic worked by most witches is done in this context: an effective person works effective magic.

It follows that witches cultivate the power of the will. Unlike Christians or Muslims, who submit themselves to the will of the God, witches attempt to develop strong wills so as to employ them effectively in magic.

But witches are seldom grim, power-obsessed fanatics. People who can write slogans such as 'How I found Goddess, and what I did to her when I found her', or issue cards identifying the bearer as 'an authentic Pope', or found societies such as the Schismatic Druids of North America, cannot be described as lacking in humour. As many witches tell me, one of the chief virtues of their religion is that it is fun. If we can ascribe to the Deity a sense of love and a sense of sympathy, why not a sense of humour?

Another doctrine held by many witches is reincarnation, which, they claim, derives from the 'Celtic/Druid/witch tradition'. In fact, reincarnation is not an important doctrine of Western religions and has little place in Celtic or Teutonic beliefs.* It is not a Druid teaching. It is, of course, a common belief in some Eastern religions, and it has been widely believed by Western occultists for over a century. The witches' belief in reincarnation derives from Gerald Gardner, who drew it out of the spiritual atmosphere of his time, particularly out of the growing vogue of Eastern religion. There is, however, a difference in the way witches regard reincarnation and the way it is traditionally perceived in Eastern religions. In the East, the soul may progress towards nirvana or sink to lower levels according to its spiritual merit. In witchcraft, the soul simply returns to earth. One witch, Cyprian, writes in his creed, 'And when my life is ended I will return to the Goddess and God in rest and strength and wisdom. When I am prepared, They will return me to my beautiful Earth to live again amongst those I love.'[70] Some other witches flatly disbelieve in reincarnation or take a tongue-in-cheek attitude towards it. As one told me, 'I used to believe in reincarnation, but that was in a previous life.'

Witches are pagans who practise magic, or magick, as Crowley and his associates spelt it. They use the term broadly. Many witches, especially those who claim to have inherited their powers, claim a high degree of psychic sensitivity. But psychic sensitivity and power can no longer be defined as magic, since what used to be called ESP, 'extrasensory perception', is now beginning to be established as a natural phenomenon.[71] Witches claim to be working with natural powers, not supernatural ones, and, as Arthur C. Clarke observed, there is little perceivable difference between magic and advanced technology. The possession of psychic powers does not necessarily make one a witch, though if one is a witch one may learn ways of directing and controlling such powers.

Witches practise a rich variety of different kinds of magic, including astrology, divination, herbology, and incantations. Divination may be worked by laying the tarot, casting the runes, gazing into crystal, holding a small pendulum, using a staff, interpreting dreams, or even necromancy. Incantations are made with an eye to the phases of the moon: positive incantations should be worked during the waxing of the moon and negative incantations when the moon is waning. The witches have developed sophisticated means of working with this principle. For example, if the intent is to cure, magic worked during the crescent moon concentrates on positive health and magic worked during the waning moon concentrates on destruction of the illness.

These varieties of magic are almost always worked to fulfil the witches' will for benign or at least morally neutral purposes. Some witches use negative magic, but they are not generally welcomed by their peers. A

*Reincarnation is not, of course, the same thing as the dying/rising fertility cycle, though some witches claim that the fertility cycle represents the renewal of the life-force.

Images stuck with pins and a sheep's heart pierced with thorns. These symbols of malevolent magic affixed to a church door, together with other incidents of grave desecration, provoked demands for the revival of witchcraft laws in Parliament in the 1960s. Most modern witches dissociate themselves from such crude rites of black magic.

number of protective spells are employed by witches against those who seek to do them magical harm. Witches do claim to be able to curse, use the evil eye, and work other negative magic, but they try to avoid using it: among other reasons, they fear retribution. Witches also insist that their magical instruments do not possess inherent powers but are merely tools to help them get in touch with their own inner powers. Only an effective person can work effective magic.

Gardner's laws state that no one can be a witch alone, because working together increases magical power. Many witches do not follow this rule and do work alone. This is certainly true of the many 'natural' or 'psychic' witches. Most neopagan witches, however, do form and enter covens in the belief that no one is really a witch unless he or she is initiated. One who wishes to enter a coven will first be given a number of pre-initiation lessons. She will learn to wipe from her mind her previous misconceptions, her Christian, Jewish, or scientist beliefs, and lies about witchcraft. She will practise techniques of meditation. She will learn to concentrate, to focus her will. She will learn to draw energy into her soul in preparation for the High Priestess' role in 'drawing down the moon', incarnating the power of the Goddess. She will learn to open up to nature by talking to a tree – and listening to its reply. She will acquire the tools of witchcraft, charge them with her own personality, and, once they are charged, many witches will not let another touch them. When ready, she will be initiated, usually at an 'esbat' (see below). Initiation ceremonies vary widely with the emphasis of the coven. Usually they include a ritual challenge and response, dedication, purification, consecration, an oath of secrecy, and formal reception. Sometimes they include a ritual kiss. In most covens and groves, degrees of membership exist through which the initiate may proceed gradually. Other covens, especially feminist ones, do not employ rank, arguing that one's power depends upon one's degree of attunement to the energy flow of the cosmos. Pre-initiation screening is careful, as the following (American) forms indicate:

---

(1) CHURCH OF WICCA (1977)

Please answer the following questions in your own words on a separate sheet of paper.

Name: Age: Birth date: Where born: Address:

Why do you want to be a Witch? What Craft or Craft-related books have you read? What are your opinions or feelings on the following: love; marriage; sex; religion; nudity; money; power? Do you enjoy being alone? Do you need people around all the time? Do you like animals? Do you have any pets? Do you enjoy being out-of-doors? Would you be willing to travel to be initiated? Would you be willing to travel to attend some of the Sabbats? Do you have a car? Do you have or can you buy or borrow a cassette recorder? What is your concept of the Devil? Is there a difference between Satanism and Witchcraft? If so, what? Do you have prejudices against blacks, Mexicans, Indians, etc? Are you married or single? If married, how does your spouse feel about the Craft? Do you know anyone in the Craft? Do you know others who are interested in learning the Craft? Do you have any problems? Do you have dreams? Do you have nightmares?

(2) NEW WICCAN CHURCH (1978)

The undersigned, being first duly sworn and under oath, does hereby state and certify:

That he/she is of full legal age and capacity or else signs this document with the full knowledge and consent of his/her parents/legal guardians.

That he/she is fully cognizant and aware of all risks of personal harm or injury inherent in his/her initiation and participation in the religion of Wicca.

That as a condition of initiation into Witchcraft the undersigned does hereby fully assume to himself/herself the risks of such harms or injuries to his/her person; does solely enter into such activities as a volunteer; and does hereby agree, warrant, and covenant to hold forever harmless from damages for personal harm or injury the New Wiccan Church, and/or any of its clergy, and/or any of its affiliates, and/or any of its chartered subsidiaries, and/or any of its officers and/or directors, and/or any of its members, and/or its authorized representatives.

That as a further condition for such initiation the undersigned further hereby agrees, warrants, and covenants not to sue or make claim against any of the aforementioned individuals, organizations, associations or entities for redress of personal injury or damage.

That he/she thoroughly and completely understands the within and foregoing and does hereby affix his/her signature below as his/her free and voluntary act and deed for the express purpose contained within the foregoing document.

DATED THIS_____Day of_____, 1978
(signed)_____
(print name) _____

(witness) _____
(witness) _____

(3) NEW WICCAN CHURCH (1978)

OATH OF SECRECY

I _____ ,

       first   *middle*   *last*

DO OF MY OWN FREE WILL AND KNOWLEDGE, WITHOUT RESERVATION, SOLEMNLY SWEAR:

1. to keep the secrets of the Craft of the Wise,

2. never to reveal the rank or identity of any Witch, without the expressed permission of that Witch,

3. never to reveal the location of the Covenstead, or any other meeting place of the Wise,

4. never to reveal the identity of any person attending such a meeting, be they Witch or not,

5. never to reveal the procedures of the Craft, the methods of working, or the manufacture and consecration of the tools,

6. never to reveal, release or permit to be revealed or released any of the writings of the Craft, written or printed, or in any other mode, i.e. photographs, tape recordings, etc., to anyone not properly vouched for by the High Priestess or High Priest,

7. never to reveal the number of Witches in any given Coven, Order, Tradition, Tribe, Confederation or Nation,

8. and I shall never misrepresent myself or another as being a Witch,

9. I shall never misrepresent the Craft of the Wise as being:

A. a parody of Christianity or any other religion.

B. in any way connected with Satanism.

C. a political organization, public or clandestine, patriotic or subversive.

Being of sound mind, and without duress, I, having reached the age of _____ years, do swear to the above conditions, recognizing the POWER OF JUST RETRIBUTION, should I ever break this solemn oath.

I fully recognize that signing this oath does not, in any way, obligate anyone in the Craft to initiate or train me, nor does this oath in any way obligate me to join this or any other Coven or Order, or obligate me to any other conditions than those stated above.

X _____   _____

                                          Date of signature

X _____   _____

                                          Date of birth

X _____ X _____

                                      Signature of Witness

Once a witch is initiated into the Craft and participates in the inner court, she will be bound by secrecy. Secrecy and exclusiveness are parts of the same pattern in the Craft. Part of the reason for secrecy is magical. Witches adopt two magical names, one of which – the coven name – they use freely in the coven and may even reveal to outsiders, the other of which they keep wholly to themselves, though sometimes it is revealed to the High Priest or Priestess or is recorded in the coven Book of Shadows. Another reason for secrecy is a well-founded fear of persecution. Witches have occasionally been subject to physical abuse by fanatics. More common are threats and intimidation. Houses have been stoned and tyres slashed. Jobs have been lost. Some Christian evangelicals, identifying witches with Satanists, have recently been increasing their hostility to the Craft both in Britain and in North America.

The secrecy of the witches is related to their exclusiveness. Exclusiveness poses a sociological problem for the Craft. Witches are few in number and would like to increase their influence by making converts. Yet generally they do not proselytize. Many come from proselytizing traditions (Christianity for example) and are rebelling against those traditions. A certain perverse pleasure in keeping secret knowledge from the profane is a part of human nature. The most important reason is that witches work in groups – the covens – and compatibility of personality is necessary to make the work of the covens effective. Insincerity, undue levity, animosity, nervous tension, and other personality problems would make it difficult to work magic or worship the gods harmoniously.

The witch uses a number of tools. The most important is the athame, a black-handled, double-edged dagger used to cast and consecrate the circle of worship and to invoke the God and Goddess. A phallic symbol, the athame also represents the power of the will. A white-handled blade may be used for carving other tools or inscribing runes. Next in importance to the athame is the chalice, the feminine symbol of receptivity, which contains the sacramental wine used as a libation. The athame is sometimes used with the chalice to represent sexual union and thus to evoke fertility, or, more generally, the broad cosmic powers generated by sexual integration. A wand, staff, or sword may be used as a phallic symbol of power and control. Candles, representing light and the transformation of matter into energy, may be used as images in the shape of a man, woman, or animal. The cauldron is another feminine symbol. The fire is usually kindled inside the cauldron rather than under it. A cord or 'cingulam' made of cords braided together is worn around the waist to signify astral binding; it may occasionally be used to measure the sacred circle. Ribbons, robes, crystals, drums, and other minor instruments may also be employed. The tools are charged with power and inscribed with a runic or other 'mystery' alphabet. One of the most important possessions of the witch is her Book of Shadows. Ideally made of parchment and leather and handmade, it may be as simple as a blank book purchased in a bookshop. The name derives from Gardner. The book contains a record of what the witch has learned in the Craft, spells, rituals, songs, and his reflections on them. Some covens maintain a Book of Shadows for community use. The individual's Book of Shadows must be destroyed at his death.

DIRK

Sexual symbols are common in witchcraft. Such symbolism is powerful in many religions, and witchcraft does not use sex in a prurient, 'nasty' fashion. Most witches are open, unrepressed, but responsible in their sexuality. Their use of sexual symbols is not pornographic but rooted in the pagan love for the earth and its growing things, and in the powerful symbol of sexual union as cosmic integration.

Witches celebrate eight major festivals or sabbats each year. The sabbat is a religious ceremony deriving from ancient European festivals celebrating seasonal or pastoral changes. The first is Yule, 20 or 21 December, celebrating the winter solstice. The next is 1 or 2 February, Oimelc, Imbolc, or Candlemas, at which initiations often take place. 20 or 21 March, Eostre, the vernal equinox, is a fertility festival. 30 April is Beltane or May Day Eve

Dirk Dykstra, *Witch Couple,* illustrating modern witches' concept of sexual union. The woman holds aloft a cup symbolizing feminine receptivity, but holds in her left hand the athame or dagger, the symbol that masculine traits also exist in her nature The man uses the opposite symbolism. The union of the sexes generates both peace and power.

Dirk Dykstra, *Wiccaning*. The wiccaning is the witches' equivalent of Christian confirmation. Note the symbols: the moon and horns of power, the candle, and the ritual cords or 'cingula'.

(transmogrified as Walpurgisnacht), and 21 June is Midsummer. 1 August is Lughnasad or Lammas, 20 or 21 September is Harvestide, and 31 October is Samhain or Hallowe'en. Some of these festivals can be considered genuine survivals rather than revivals: Beltane was celebrated in living memory in certain Scottish and northern English villages, and Hallowe'en has a long and celebrated history. Many witches alter the dates of the festivals to conform to their own seasons. In the southern hemisphere, for example, the dates are usually reversed, and in California, where the land is green in winter and dry and dead in summer, the dates are sometimes modified. Often a festival or sabbat will be deferred to the following weekend or other convenient time. The sabbats are open to prospective new members and exist for worship, celebration, and socializing. In addition to these more informal sabbats, witches hold closed meetings limited to initiates; these are generally called 'esbats'.* The esbats are held weekly, or at full and new moon, or at whatever intervals the coven feels appropriate.

A typical witches' meeting will begin with a 'gathering' or informal reception, during which people express their thoughts and feelings openly. Some meetings are held 'skyclad' – naked – others are held robed. At some the participants may choose individually whether to be naked or robed. The

*The term 'esbat' is dubious. It was taken from De Lancre by Margaret Murray, who then derived it from the French *s'esbattre*, which she translated as 'to frolic'. It does not appear in any medieval or early modern document.

California covens meet 'skyclad' to celebrate a yearly festival in the mountains.

tradition of nakedness derives both from *Aradia* and from Gardner. Explanations vary. Some witches say that it increases their contact with the powers of nature, others that it erases class distinctions, others that they wish to appear before the gods as they were born, with nothing to hide, and still others that it gives them a salutary sense of freedom. The witches prepare themselves for the meeting by meditation and often by bathing and anointing. The meeting may be held in any private place, but whenever possible a sabbat or major festival is held outdoors and in a lonely place. The altar is prepared. The arrangement of the altar varies considerably from coven to coven, but it usually holds a statue of the Goddess (and horned god), candles for fire, a chalice for water or wine, a thurible for air, a container of salt or a pentacle paten for earth, and an athame, sword, and/or wand.

The nine-foot magical circle is measured and cast with the athame or sword. Often a pentagram is cast within the circle. Witches emphasize the difference between their circle and that of the ceremonial magician. The magician will draw his circle and stay within it in order to protect himself from the powers that roam outside its protecting bounds. The witch uses the circle to concentrate the cosmic powers within it and may, with precautions and at the proper times, go in and out of the circle without fear. The witches' circle is a sacred space, a place between the world of humans and the world of the gods. A place of contact between two realities, it is also a place where humans may unite with the archetypes and the gods, becoming the cosmic forces and drawing strength from them. The circle is also, as Aidan Kelly puts it, a reservoir holding the energy raised in the ritual until the time comes to release it. The circle has four cardinal points, north (associated with earth), south (with fire), west (water), and east (air). When the circle is cast, the Lords of the Towers (guardian spirits) of each of the cardinal points are evoked, and the circle is consecrated. (These correspondences vary from coven to coven.)

Above left: George Patterson, a California witch and founder of the Georgian branch of witchcraft.

Above right: the magic circle in the garden of George Patterson.

The Goddess (and God) are invoked with ritual words and/or poetry. The Priestess now 'draws down the moon', that is, she dances, sings, meditates, or does whatever is most effective in opening herself to divine power. She alters her consciousness and receives into herself the power and being of the Goddess, in a sense becoming the Goddess. Next the coven raises the cone of power. This is the combined will of the group, 'intensified through ritual and meditative techniques, focused toward an end collectively agreed upon.'[72] The members of the coven join hands and sing and dance in a circle. The High Priestess stands in the centre of the circle. When she feels the energy reach its peak, she knows that the cone of power has been raised. She signals for the coven to let go the power, focuses it with her will, and speeds it towards its destination. A few covens sometimes practise ritual sex to intensify the magical power raised in the cone, but this is rare. The cone may be directed towards a spiritual and general end or towards a quite specific earthly purpose. Often the cone may be sent to heal the sick or to achieve some other good mutually willed by the coven.

The raising and release of the cone requires a great outpouring of energy, and this part of the ritual is followed by a period of meditation and centring, after which the coven takes communion with cakes and wine which the Priestess (or Priest) has consecrated by dipping an athame or wand into the chalice and touching the cakes with other sacred tools. The cakes and cup are passed with a kiss from Priestess to Priest, from Priest to Maiden, from Maiden to Summoner, and so round the coven, man to woman, woman to man, till all have partaken. After communion ensues an informal, unstructured period for poetry, discussion, minor magic, songs, games, or whatever seems appropriate. The rite is now almost over, but the circle must be broken, the sacred space returned to the mundane, and the Priestess brought back from her union with the divine. The guardian spirits and deities must be thanked. The Priestess breaks the circle by cutting across its circumference with the tip of the sword, wand, or athame. The coven members return to their ordinary lives as housewives, students, bankers, librarians, or computer technologists.

There are perhaps twenty to a hundred thousand neopagan witches in the world. Since many witches prefer – or insist upon – anonymity, no accurate estimate is possible, but the numbers are growing. Witchcraft is still predominantly a white, middle-class movement, and most witches are relatively well educated. Women outnumber men by about two to one, and this imbalance may be growing because of the increase in feminine witchcraft. Class distinctions are less evident in feminist groups. Most witches are in their teens, twenties, or thirties, and most are urban, as is usually true of those who love nature (the farmers are too busy fighting it). Most witches I know are unusual only by being extraordinary in their creativity and independence. They differ from many who follow Eastern religions in their independence of gurus and their desire to take responsibility for their lives into their own hands. They have become pagans because they are able to use their dramatic, artistic, and poetic powers in the Craft, because they find in the Craft a sense of beauty, joy, and freedom, because they gain emotional growth and satisfaction from it, because they love nature and the wild, because they find a strong sense of community in their covens, and, if they are women, because they want a religion free of patriarchy and hierarchy.

Behind the details of their rituals and practices is the essence of the Craft. All witchcraft rituals work within the basic matter/energy structure of the cosmos. None are believed to be supernatural. To work magic one must be in touch with the energy flow of the cosmos and move with it, shaping it gently and respectfully to your ends as you move. The ritual circle is the focus of that energy. Thus each member of the coven needs to be totally present, totally open to the cosmic powers, to be able to concentrate their will, to be psychologically 'together' and not distracted, and to be able to work harmoniously with the other members of the coven. Almost all witches emphasize that the centre of witchcraft is the sense of freedom, of openness to the cosmic and the divine, of access to the unconscious and the archetypes, and the exercise of mythopoeic creativity. Witchcraft is not necessarily anti-rational, but it taps wisdom and knowledge that are non-rational. As one witch put it, 'if the rituals work for you they are good; if not, they are useless.' And another witch told Margot Adler:

I'm in the Craft because it feels right. I'm a visionary. The Craft is a place for visionaries. I love myth, dream, visionary art. The Craft is a place where all of these things fit together: beauty, pageantry, music, dance, song, dream. It's necessary to me, somehow. It's almost like food and drink.

10 The role of witchcraft

Historically the three types of witch are: the sorcerer who practises the simple magic found worldwide; the heretic who allegedly practised diabolism and was prosecuted during the witch-craze; the modern neopagan. Great differences separate them; they have in common the name of witch and the practice of magic.

Of the three varieties of witchcraft, that of the witch-craze has had the greatest effect historically. Historical European witchcraft was a diabolism formed out of ancient sorcery, paganism, folklore, heresy, scholastic theology, and inquisitorial trials. Whether this kind of witchcraft ever actually existed is open to question. A few individuals and groups may have practised something like diabolical rites, but these were probably rare. The chief importance of heretical witchcraft is the concept: what the witches really did is eclipsed by what they were believed to do. People act on the basis of what they believe to be true, and the concept of witchcraft brought about the deaths of hundreds of thousands of men and women, terrorized millions, defiled the minds of the best thinkers for centuries, and left a hideous blot on the record of Christian society.

Much has been said about the reasons for the origins, the spread, and the ultimate decline of the witch-craze. But the fundamental importance of the craze is not its particular social and intellectual genesis. The witch-craze is essentially not the fault of the Middle Ages or of Christianity, nor of Aristotelianism or of Renaissance magic. Fundamentally, the witch-craze was one particular form of a flaw in human nature, the desire of human beings to project evil on others, define them as outsiders, and then punish them horribly. The burnings at Bamberg and the hangings at Salem are functionally and structurally comparable to the ovens of Dachau, the massacre of My Lai, and the brutalities of the Gulag. The ideology determines the form the evil takes, but the evil lurking behind the form is independent of ideologies.

To turn from heretical witchcraft to neopagan witchcraft is refreshing. Contrary to what many people suppose, modern witches do not worship the Devil, say black masses, or practise orgies. A very few people calling themselves witches do some of these things, but they stand quite outside what is becoming an increasingly defined tradition, and they are no more relevant to the mainstream of modern witchcraft than some bizarre Christian sects are relevant to the mainstream of Christianity. The mainstream of modern witchcraft is the conscious revival of paganism and magic. What is the reason for the increasing success of witchcraft, and what is its religious validity?

The success of witchcraft is partly explainable in terms of the general growth of the occult in recent years. In a broad historical view, interest in the occult has grown rapidly in periods of rapid social breakdown, when establishments cease to provide readily accepted answers and people turn elsewhere for assurance. The third century AD, when Roman society was weakening, the fifteenth and sixteenth centuries AD, when the medieval synthesis was crumbling, and the twentieth century AD are periods for which this generalization seems true. The roots of the current occult revival are in the soil of the late nineteenth and early twentieth centuries, when traditional Christianity was weakening. Since the so-called Aquarian conjunction of 5 February 1962 (the great conjunction of five planets and the sun and moon within the sign of Aquarius on that day), the occult has gained enormously. Many observers, including some occultists, believe that the current interest is a fad, and in fact interest has waned somewhat since its peak in the 1968–73 period. But one has only to look at the substantial sections on the occult in bookshops to see that interest continues to be high.

It is difficult to define the occult, and many phenomena formerly defined as occult, such as ESP, are gaining scientific respectability, as we have seen. But consider a number of popular phenomena and what they have in common: in the theatre, *Hair*, with the enormous effect of its Aquarian ideas on a whole generation; in the cinema, *Rosemary's Baby*, *The Exorcist*, *Close Encounters*, and their imitators; in books, the colourful successes of Von Däniken and Castañeda, and the explosion of interest in Tolkien and other science fiction and fantasy; wide belief in astrology; the UFO phenomenon; and the apparently permanent presence of hallucinogens on the social scene. Intellectuals, especially the university establishments, have for the most part struggled against this tide, and the most powerful current in universities today continues to be the move toward positivism and quantification. But an undercurrent has been rising for a decade. In psychology, behaviourists are still in power but begin to find themselves undercut by humanists and eclectics. In philosophy, logical positivism is facing a number of challengers. Physiological psychology has recently investigated the creative, intuitive, and mythopoeic powers of the right brain as opposed to the analytical left brain. The ideas of C. G. Jung and Mircea Eliade on the essential importance of mythology to the human mind are gradually transforming religious, psychological, and philosophical assumptions. As for witchcraft itself, the majority of universities and colleges have now offered public lectures on the subject, and the degree of scholarly interest it has generated can be seen in the bibliography of this book. In the main, historians have naturally emphasized historical, rather than modern, witchcraft, but as modern witchcraft grows this will of necessity change.

The cracking of religious and scientific orthodoxies allows scope for the formation of alternative ways of looking at the world. Many efforts in this direction are bound to be ignorant and uncritical. Indeed, lack of basic critical standards is characteristic of what is called the occult. Earlier I defined superstition as a belief held by an individual who does not have a coherent system of thought in which that belief appropriately fits. By this definition much occult thought is undeniably superstitious. Occultists often adopt beliefs according to the following pattern: It could be; I want it to be;

therefore it must be. Such non-thought is ultimately self-destructive. Both dogmatic rigidity and uncritical credulity impede the search for truth.

The occult has often taken ignorant anti-historical and anti-critical positions in order to defend preconceived, neurotic superstitions. Insofar as it does this, it poses at least a mild threat. The term 'occult' is probably too closely associated with this kind of position to be able to acquire – or deserve – more positive connotations. But if we replace the vague and negative concept of the occult with the concept of creative, synthetic approaches to reality then a positive view is appropriate. One of the most patently false ideas cherished in academic communities and in society in general is the idea of progress, particularly progress linked to scientific advances. The idea of progress, which is scientifically dubious in terms of the law of entropy and absurd historically, has fixed a number of strange notions in our minds. We believe that 'savage societies' progress to become civilizations. We believe that analytic thought represents progress over synthetic thought. We have been taught by positivists that magic progressed into religion and religion progressed into science. We believe that polytheism progressed into monotheism and monotheism into atheism. We believe that exploitation of nature represents progress over concord with nature. Once these untenable notions are removed, we are rendered capable of seeing the value in alternatives that we have rigidly rejected. Perhaps syncretic, intuitive thought is as valuable as analytic thought. Perhaps atheism is not an advance over religion. Perhaps polytheism can help us get at truths monotheism has lost.

It is in this context that modern witchcraft can be seen, not as a bizarre aberration, but as a potentially valuable approach to reality. Academics dismiss witchcraft as nonsense, Christians shun it as evil, and most people prefer to think that it simply doesn't exist. What some witches have to say is in fact silly, and encountering such ideas on his first exposure to witchcraft, an intelligent person is likely to dismiss it hastily. A further danger in witchcraft is that unstable people may be led into destructive or self-destructive acts by exposure to magic. My own view of witchcraft was initially extremely negative after two students in one of my classes performed a home-made occult rite in which they nearly bled to death. But silly talk or irrational behaviour on the part of a few witches proves no more than silliness or irrationality on the part of a few Christians or a few atheists. The question rather is whether witchcraft has anything of value to offer us. I think it does. As one writer put it, 'The practice of the art and the craft is not as dangerous as our credulous Christian critics contend, but neither is it as frivolously dysfunctional as Cartesian pedants would suppose.'[73]

One need not be a witch – I am not – to understand witchcraft as a valid expression of the religious experience. The religion of witchcraft offers to restore a lost option, paganism, to our religious world view. Both Christianity and scientism have taught us falsely that paganism is nonsense. We are taught that pagans worshipped idols, that they believed undignified things about a useless variety of silly gods, and that they invented interesting but irrelevant myths. One might respectably be a Protestant, Catholic, or Jew, or even a Buddhist, but one could certainly not be a pagan. This is not an informed view. The religions of Egypt and Canaan, of the Celts and the

Teutons, when properly understood, are rich, sophisticated, beautiful, and psychologically full of insight. The neopagan witches are attempting to re-create the positive values of pagan religion.

These values include an emphasis upon individual creativity and expression in moulding rites and beliefs. Neopagan witchcraft and its rites provide a great deal of room for poetry, dance, music, laughter, and whatever the moment and the tradition inspire. Witchcraft encourages an openness to the awe of the natural world and reverence and love of the cosmos. For this reason, North American witches have drawn close to native American (Indian) religion. Witchcraft also offers a grasp of the importance of the unconscious in integrating the whole psyche; and a sophisticated understanding of meditation. Most importantly it offers a sense of the importance of the feminine principle, almost completely lost in the masculine symbolism of the great monotheistic religions; and a sense of variety and diversity in the Godhead. The validity of polytheism has recently been argued in theology and will increasingly be argued as the progressive fallacy that monotheism is necessarily an improvement over polytheism is discarded.[74]

Whatever the future of witchcraft as a religious force of its own, these values, so often forgotten and neglected in Western society, should be reintroduced as freshly as possible. It is not possible to worship the old gods as if two thousand years of Christianity and science had not altered our world view, but the old gods have much to say again. And what they are saying is an exciting synthesis of ancient beliefs and new ideas, a synthesis that has something new and vital to offer. Polytheism and feminism are two ancient religious ideas whose time has come – again.

Sorcery persists; diabolical witchcraft is almost dead; modern witches create a new religion. Witchcraft is not a coherent concept but a term covering a variety of phenomena only loosely linked. But for good or ill, magic continues to appeal, and witchcraft will not soon vanish from this earth.

THE MEANING OF THE WORD 'WITCH'

The ultimate origin of the English word 'witch' is the Indo-European root
weik², which has to do with religion and magic. *Weik²* produced four
families of derivatives: 1. *wih-l*, which yielded Old English *wigle*, 'sorcery',
and *wiglera*, 'sorcerer', and, through Old and Middle French, modern English
'guile'. Also Old English *wil*, Middle and modern English 'wile'. 2. Old
Norse *wihl-*, 'craftiness'. 3. *wik-*, 'holy', whence Old High German *wihen*
and German *weihen*, 'to consecrate', Middle High German *wich*, 'holy', and
Latin *victima*, 'sacrifice'. 4. *wikk-*, 'magic, sorcery', whence Middle German
wikken, 'to predict', and Old English *wicca*, *wicce*, 'witch', and *wiccian*, 'to
work sorcery, bewitch'. From *wicca* derives Middle English *witche* and modern
'witch'.

Different from *weik²* and its derivations is *weik⁴*, 'bending', whence Old
English *wican*, 'to bend', from which the modern English 'weak' and 'witch-
elm'. Related to *wican* are Old Saxon *wikan*, Old High German *wichan*, Old
Norse *vikja*, all meaning 'to bend, or turn aside'.

Old English *witan*, 'to know', and all related words including 'wise' are
totally unrelated to either of the above.

Notes on the text

Introduction

1 Lucy Mair, *Witchcraft* (New York 1969), p. 211.
2 Mair 1969, p. 204.
3 Paul Boyer and Stephen Nissenbaum, *Salem Possessed* (Cambridge [Mass.] 1974), pp. xi–xii.
4 For a presentation of the history of concepts, see my book *The Devil* (Ithaca and London 1977).

Chapter 1

5 E. E. Evans-Pritchard, *Witchcraft, Oracles, and Magic among the Azande*, 2nd edn (Oxford 1950), pp. 63–4.
6 Geoffrey Parrinder, *Witchcraft: European and African* (London 1958), p. 133.
7 Parrinder 1958, p. 138; Jeffrey B. Russell, *Witchcraft in the Middle Ages* (Ithaca and London 1972), pp. 13–15.
8 Mair 1969, p. 81.
9 Mair 1969, p. 86.
10 Alfred Métraux, *Voodoo in Haiti*, 2nd edn (New York 1972), p. 4.
11 Métraux 1972, p. 323.
12 Métraux 1972, p. 43.
13 Métraux 1972, p. 49.
14 Georges Contenau, *Everyday Life in Babylonia and Assyria* (London 1959), p. 255.

Chapter 2

15 Elliot Rose, *A Razor for a Goat* (Toronto 1962), pp. 64, 79.
16 Preceding four quotations about Anglo-Saxon magic: Godfrid Storms, *Anglo-Saxon Magic* (The Hague 1948), pp. 54, 65, 247 and 261.
17 John R. McNeill and Helena M. Gamer, *Medieval Handbooks of Penance* (New York 1938), pp. 198, 246.
18 Marie-Louise von Franz, *Shadow and Evil in Fairytales* (Zurich 1974), pp. 163–4.
19 Jeffrey B. Russell, *Witchcraft in the Middle Ages* (Ithaca and London 1972), p. 67.
20 Russell 1972, p. 75.
21 Russell 1972, pp. 76–7; 291–3.

Chapter 3

22 Grado J. Merlo, *Eretici e Inquisitori* (Turin 1977), pp. 27–36.
23 Walter Wakefield and Austin P. Evans, *Heresies of the High Middle Ages* (New York 1969), p. 254.
24 Merlo 1977, p. 65.

Chapter 4

25 William of Malmesbury, *De Gestis Regum Anglorum*, ed. W. Stubbs, 2 vols., (London 1887–9); vol. I, pp. 253–5.
26 Carlo Ginzburg, *I benandanti . . .* (Turin 1966).
27 Richard Kieckhefer, *European Witch Trials: their Foundation in Popular and Learned Culture 1300–1500* (Berkeley and Los Angeles 1976).
28 Etienne Delcambre, *Le concept de la sorcellerie dans le Duché de Lorraine au XVIème et XVIIème siècle*, (Nancy 1948).
29 Rossell Hope Robbins, *Encyclopaedia of Witchcraft and Demonology* (New York 1959), p. 489.
30 Robbins 1959, pp. 106–7.
31 E. William Monter, *Witchcraft in France and Switzerland* (Ithaca and London 1976), pp. 195–6.
32 E. William Monter, *European Witchcraft* (New York 1969), pp. 75–81.
33 George Lincoln Burr, ed., 'The Witch-Persecution at Bamberg', *Translations and Reprints from Original Sources of European History*, vol. 3 (University of Pennsylvania 1896), pp. 23–8.
34 Robbins 1959, pp. 312–17.

Chapter 5

35 A. D. F. Macfarlane, *Witchcraft in Tudor and Stuart England* (London 1970), pp. 82–4.
36 Robbins 1959, p. 359.
37 Robbins 1959, p. 252.
38 Robbins 1959, p. 232.
39 Keith Thomas, *Religion and the Decline of Magic* (London 1971), p. 523.
40 Boyer and Nissenbaum 1974, p. 3.

41 Boyer and Nissenbaum 1974, p. 5.
42 Boyer and Nissenbaum 1974, p. 10.
43 Boyer and Nissenbaum 1974, p. 11.

CHAPTER 6

44 Macfarlane 1970, pp. 178–82.
45 *Malleus Maleficarum*, trans. Montague Summers (London 1928), pp. 43–6.
46 Boyer and Nissenbaum 1974, pp. 26–7.
47 Boyer and Nissenbaum 1974, p. 30.
48 Boyer and Nissenbaum 1974, pp. 103–4.
49 Boyer and Nissenbaum 1974, p. 69.
50 Boyer and Nissenbaum 1974, p. 177.
51 H.R. Trevor-Roper, *The European Witch-Craze of the Sixteenth and Seventeenth Centuries and Other Essays* (London and New York 1969), p. 190.

CHAPTER 7

52 Macfarlane 1970, p. 202.

CHAPTER 8

53 Jean Tyson in *The Atlanta Journal*, 23 June 1978.
54 Hans Sebald, *Witchcraft: the Heritage of a Heresy* (New York 1978), p. 223.
55 Sebald 1978, pp. 100–101.
56 Burton Wolfe, introduction to Anton Szandor LaVey, *The Satanic Bible* (New York 1969), p. 18.
57 LaVey 1969, p. 21.
58 LaVey 1969, p. 53.

59 LaVey 1969, p. 110.
60 LaVey 1969, p. 17.
61 Vincent Bugliosi, *Helter Skelter* (New York 1974), p. 175.
62 Bugliosi 1974, p. 177.

CHAPTER 9

63 Charles Leland, *Aradia* (New York 1899), p. vii. Italics added.
64 From 'Statement of Intention', part of the teaching materials from the class 'Women, Goddesses, and Homemade Religion', Fall 1974, by Barbry MyOwn. Supplied by Deborah Bender.
65 Candice Haddad Campbell, 'Evocation of the Goddess' (n.d.).
66 Tony Kelly, 'Pagan Musings' (n.d.).
67 H.J. Rose, *Religion in Greece and Rome* (New York 1957), p. xii.
68 Jeffrey B. Russell, *The Devil* (Ithaca and London 1977), pp. 34, 58, 134.
69 Houston Roberts, pers. comm.
70 Houston Roberts, pers. comm.
71 See C. T. Tart, *PSI: Scientific Studies of the Psychic Realm* (New York 1977).
72 Margot Adler.

CHAPTER 10

73 C.L. Runyon, 'Magick and hypnosis', *Gnostica*, 5 (1977), p. 23.
74 David Miller, *The New Polytheism* (New York 1974).

Bibliography

Adler, Margot. *Drawing down the Moon: the Resurgence of Paganism in America*, New York (forthcoming).

Anglo, Sydney, ed. *The Damned Art: Essays in the Literature of Witchcraft*, London 1977.

Ardener, Edwin. 'Witchcraft, Economics, and the Continuity of Belief', in Mary Douglas, ed., *Witchcraft: Confessions and Accusations*, London 1970.

Barb, Alfons A. 'The Survival of Magic Arts', in Arnaldo Momigliano, ed., *The Conflict between Paganism and Christianity in the Fourth Century*, Oxford 1963.

Bonewits, Philip E. I. *Real Magic*, 2nd edn, Berkeley 1979.

Bouisson, Maurice. *Magic: its History and Principal Rites*, New York 1961.

Boyer, Paul, and Stephen Nissenbaum. *Salem Possessed: the Social Origins of Witchcraft*, Cambridge [Mass.] 1974.

— *Salem-Village Witchcraft: a Documentary Record of Local Conflict in Colonial New England*, Belmont, California 1972.

Brian, Robert. 'Child-witches', in Mary Douglas, ed., *Witchcraft: Confessions and Accusations*, London 1970.

Briggs, Katharine M. *Pale Hecate's Team: an Examination of the Beliefs on Witchcraft and Magic among Shakespeare's Contemporaries and his Immediate Successors*, London and New York 1962.

Brown, Peter. 'Sorcery, Demons, and the Rise of Christianity: from Late Antiquity to the Middle Ages', in Peter Brown, *Religion and Society in the Age of Saint Augustine*, London and New York 1972.

Brucker, Gene A. 'Sorcery in Early Renaissance Florence', *Studies in the Renaissance*, 10 (1963), 7–24.

Bryant, Alfred T. *Zulu Medicine and Medicine-men*, Cape Town 1966.

Caro Baroja, Julio. *Vidas Mágicas e Inquisición*, 2 vols., Madrid 1967.

— *The World of the Witches*, London 1964.

Cavendish, Richard. *The Black Arts*, New York and London 1967.

Clark, Stuart, and P. T. J. Morgan. 'Religion and Magic in Elizabethan Wales: Robert Holland's Dialogue on Witchcraft', *Journal of Ecclesiastical History*, 27 (1976), 31–46.

Cohn, Norman. *Europe's Inner Demons: an Enquiry Inspired by the Great Witch-hunt*, London and New York 1975.

— 'The Myth of Satan and his Human Servants', in Mary Douglas, ed., *Witchcraft: Confessions and Accusations*, London 1970.

Crowe, Martha J., ed. *Witchcraft: Catalogue of the Witchcraft Collection in Cornell University Library*, with introduction by Rossell Hope Robbins, Millwood, N.Y., 1977.

Crowther, Patricia. *Witchcraft in Yorkshire*, Clapham [Yorks.] 1973.

Douglas, Mary. 'Thirty years after *Witchcraft, Oracles, and Magic*', in Douglas, ed., *Witchcraft: Confessions and Accusations*, London 1970.

— ed. *Witchcraft: Confessions and Accusations*, London 1970.

Dunlap, Rhodes. 'King James and some Witches: the Date and Text of the *Daemonologie*', *Philological Quarterly*, 54 (1975), 40–46.

Ehrenreich, Barbara, and Deirdre English. *Witches, Midwives, and Nurses: a History of Women Healers*, 2nd edn, New York 1972.

Eliade, Mircea. 'Some Observations on European Witchcraft', *History of Religions*, 14 (1975), 149–72.

— *Occultism, Witchcraft, and Cultural Fashions: Essays in Comparative Religions*, Chicago and London 1976.

Evans-Pritchard, Edward E. *Witchcraft, Oracles, and Magic among the Azande*, 2nd edn, Oxford 1950.

Eyre, Kathleen. *Witchcraft in Lancashire*, Clapham [Yorks.] 1974.

Fortune, Reo F. *Sorcerers of Dobu: the Social Anthropology of the Dobu Islanders of the Western Pacific*, London and New York 1963.

Gardner, Gerald B. *Witchcraft Today*, London 1954.

Gibson, Walter B. *Witchcraft*, London and New York 1973.

Ginzburg, Carlo. *I benandanti: ricerche sulla stregoneria e sui culti agrari tra cinquecento e seicento*, Turin 1966.

Graves, Robert. *The White Goddess*, New York 1948.

Greeley, Andrew M. *The Mary Myth: on the Femininity of God*, New York 1977.

Grigulewic, J. R. *Ketzer, Hexen, Inquisitoren: Geschichte der Inquisition, 13.–20. Jahrhundert*, Berlin 1976.

Hansen, Chadwick. *Witchcraft at Salem*, New York 1969.

Hansen, Joseph, ed. *Quellen und Untersuchungen zur Geschichte des Hexenwahns und der Hexenverfolgung im Mittelalter*, Bonn 1901.

— *Zauberwahn, Inquisition, und Hexenprozess im Mittelalter, und die Entstehung der grossen Hexenverfolgung*, Munich 1900.

Harvey, Margaret. 'Papal Witchcraft: the Charges against Benedict XIII', in Derek Baker, ed., *Sanctity and Secularity: the Church and the World*, Oxford 1973.

Henningsen, Gustav. *The European Witch-persecution*, Copenhagen 1973.

Hole, Christina. *Witchcraft in England*, London 1945.

Holzer, Hans. *The Truth about Witchcraft*, New York 1969.

Jensen, Peter F. 'Calvin and witchcraft', *Reformed Theological Review*, 34 (1975), 76–86.

Johns, June. *King of the Witches: the World of Alex Sanders*, New York 1969.

Jones, William R. 'Political Uses of Sorcery in Medieval Europe', *The Historian*, 34 (1972), 670–87.

Kelly, Aidan. *The Rebirth of Witchcraft: Tradition and Creativity in the Gardnerian Reform*, forthcoming.

Kelly, Henry Ansgar. *The Devil, Demonology, and Witchcraft: the Development of Christian Beliefs in Evil Spirits*, 2nd edn, Garden City, N.Y., 1974.

— 'English kings and the fear of sorcery', *Mediaeval Studies*, 39 (1977), 206–38.

Kieckhefer, Richard. *European Witch Trials: their Foundations in Popular and Learned Culture, 1300–1500*, Berkeley and Los Angeles 1976.

Kittredge, George Lyman. *Witchcraft in Old and New England*, Cambridge [Mass.] 1929.

Kluckhohn, Clyde. *Navaho Witchcraft*, Cambridge [Mass.] 1944.

Kors, Alan C., and Edward Peters, eds. *Witchcraft in Europe, 1100–1700: a Documentary History*, Philadelphia 1972, London 1973.

Kruse, Johann. *Hexen unter uns?*, 2nd edn, Leer 1978.

Lambert, Malcolm. *Medieval Heresy: Popular Movements from Bogomil to Hus*, London 1977.

Lea, Henry Charles. *Materials Toward a History of Witchcraft*, 3 vols., New York 1957.

Leek, Sibyl. *The Complete Art of Witchcraft*, London and New York 1971.

Leland, Charles A. *Aradia, or the Gospel of the Witches*, New York 1899.

Leutenbauer, Siegfried. *Hexerei- und Zaubereidelikt in der Literatur von 1450 bis 1550*, Berlin 1972.

Lewis, Joan M. 'A structural approach to witchcraft and spirit-possession', in Mary Douglas, ed., *Witchcraft: Confessions and Accusations*, London 1970.

Lyman, Stanford M. *The Seven Deadly Sins: Society and Evil*, New York 1978.

Macfarlane, Alan D.J. *Witchcraft in Tudor and Stuart England: a Regional and Comparative Study*, London and New York 1970.

Mair, Lucy. *Witchcraft*, London, New York and Toronto 1969.

Malinowski, Bronislaw. *Magic, Science, and Religion, and Other Essays*, Boston 1948.

Manselli, Raoul. *Magia e stregoneria nel medio evo*, Turin 1976.

— 'Le premesse medioevali della caccia alle streghe', in Marina Romanello, ed., *La stregoneria in Europa (1450–1650)*, Bologna 1975.

Maple, Eric. *The Dark World of the Witches*, New York 1964.

Martello, Leo Louis. *Witchcraft: the Old Religion*, Secaucus, N.J., 1973.

Marwick, Max G. 'Another Modern Anti-witchcraft Movement in East Central Africa', *Africa*, 20 (1950), 100–112.

— *Sorcery in its Social Setting: a Study of the Northern Rhodesian Cewâ*, Manchester and New York 1965.

— *Witchcraft and Sorcery*, Baltimore 1970.

Masters, Robert E.L. *Eros and Evil: the Sexual Psychopathology of Witchcraft*, New York 1962.

Merzbacher, Friedrich. *Die Hexenprozesse in Franken*, 2nd edn, Munich 1970.

Métraux, Alfred. *Voodoo in Haiti*, 2nd edn, New York 1972.

Middleton, John, ed. *Magic, Witchcraft, and Curing*, Garden City 1967.

— and E.H. Winter, eds. *Witchcraft and Sorcery in East Africa*, London and New York 1963.

Midelfort, H.C. Erik. 'Recent Witch-hunting Research, or Where do we go from here?', *The Papers of the Bibliographic Society of America*, 62 (1968), 373–420.

— *Witch-hunting in Southwestern Germany, 1562–1684: the Social and Intellectual Foundations*, Stanford 1972.

Monter, E. William, ed. *European Witchcraft*, New York 1969.

— 'The Historiography of European Witchcraft: Progress and Prospects', *Journal of Interdisciplinary History*, 2 (1972), 435–51.

— 'The Pedestal and the Stake: Courtly Love and Witchcraft', in Renate Bridenthal and Claudia Koonz, eds., *Becoming Visible: Women in European History*, Boston 1977.

— *Witchcraft in France and Switzerland: the Borderlands during the Reformation*, Ithaca and London 1976.

Murray, Alexander. 'Medieval Origins of the Witch Hunt', *The Cambridge Quarterly*, 7 (1976), 63–74.

Murray, Margaret A. *The Witch-cult in Western Europe: a Study in Anthropology*, Oxford 1921.

Newall, Venetia, ed. *The Witch Figure*, London 1973.

Notestein, Wallace. *History of Witchcraft in England from 1558–1718*, Washington 1911.

Nugent, Donald. 'The Renaissance . . . of Witchcraft', *Church History*, 40 (1971), 69–78.

Oesterreich, Traugott K. *Possession, Demoniacal and Other: among Primitive Races, in Antiquity, the Middle Ages, and Modern Times*, London and New York 1930.

Parrinder, Geoffrey. *Witchcraft: European and African*, 3rd edn, London 1970.

Peters, Edward. *The Magician, the Witch, and the Law*, Philadelphia 1978.

Reynolds, Barrie. *Magic, Divination, and Witchcraft among the Barotse of Northern Rhodesia*, Berkeley and London 1963.

Rhodes, Henry T.F. *The Satanic Mass*, London 1954.

Robbins, Rossell H. *The Encyclopaedia of Witchcraft and Demonology*, New York 1959.

— 'The Heresy of witchcraft', *The South Atlantic Quarterly*, 65 (1966), 532–43.

— 'Pandaemonium and the Sadducees', *Thought*, 52 (1977), 167–87.

— 'Yellow Cross and Green Faggot', *The Cornell Library Journal* (1970), 3–33.

Romanello, Marina, ed. *La stregoneria in Europa (1450–1650)*, Bologna 1975.

Rose, Elliot. *A Razor for a Goat: a Discussion of Certain Problems in the History of Witchcraft and Diabolism*, Toronto 1962.

Rosen, Barbara, ed. *Witchcraft*, London 1969.

Rosen, George. 'A Study of the Persecution of Witches in Europe as a Contribution to the Understanding of Mass Delusions and Psychic Epidemics', *Journal of Health and Human Behavior*, 1 (1960), 200–211.

Ruel, Malcolm. 'Were-animals and the Introverted Witch', in Mary Douglas, ed., *Witchcraft: Confessions and Accusations*, London 1970.

Runeberg, Arne. *Witches, Demons, and Fertility Magic: Analysis of their Significance and Mutual Relations in West-European folk religion*, Helsinki 1947.

Rush, John A. *Witchcraft and Sorcery: an Anthropological Perspective of the Occult*, Springfield, Ill., 1974.

Russell, Jeffrey Burton. *The Devil: Perceptions of Evil from Antiquity to Primitive Christianity*, Ithaca and London 1977.

— 'Medieval Witchcraft and Medieval Heresy', in Edward A. Tiryakin, ed., *On the Margin of the Visible: Sociology, the Esoteric, and the Occult*, New York 1974.

— 'Witchcraft and Heresies', *Values and the Medieval Classics in Secondary Education*, Spartanburg, S.C., 1969.

— *Witchcraft in the Middle Ages*, Ithaca and London 1972.

— and Mark Wyndham. 'Witchcraft and the demonization of heresy', *Mediaevalia*, 2 (1976), 1–21.

Sebald, Hans. *Witchcraft: the Heritage of a Heresy*, New York 1978.

Starkey, Marion L. *The Devil in Massachusetts: a Modern Inquiry into the Salem Witch Trials*, New York 1949.

Storms, Godfrid. *Anglo-Saxon Magic*, The Hague 1948.

Symonds, John. *The Great Beast*, New York 1952.

— *The Magic of Aleister Crowley*, London 1958.

Thomas, Keith. *Religion and the Decline of Magic*, London and New York 1971.

Thorndike, Lynn. *A History of Magic and Experimental Science*, 8 vols., New York 1923–58.

Trevor-Roper, Hugh. *The European Witch-craze of the Sixteenth and Seventeenth Centuries and other Essays*, London and New York 1956.

Truzzi, Marcello. 'The Occult Revival as Popular Culture: some Random Observations on the Old and Nouveau Witch', *Sociological Quarterly*, 13 (1972), 16–36.

Valiente, Doreen. *ABC of Witchcraft*, New York 1973.

— *Natural Magic*, New York 1975.

— *Witchcraft for Tomorrow*, London 1978.

Webster, Hutton. *Magic: a Sociological Study*, Stanford 1948.

West, Robert H. 'Some Popular Literature of Witchcraft since 1969', *The Review of Politics*, 37 (1975), 547–56.

Woods, Ricard. *The Devil*, Chicago 1973.

— *The Occult Revolution: a Christian Meditation*, New York 1971.

Yates, Frances. *Giordano Bruno and the Hermetic Tradition*, London 1964.

Ziegeler, Wolfgang. *Möglichkeiten der Kritik am Hexen- und Zauberwesen im ausgehenden Mittelalter: zeitgenössische Stimmen und ihre soziale Zugehörigkeit*, Cologne and Vienna 1973.

List of illustrations

Frontispiece
    Brujos por el Aire. Oil painting by Francisco Goya, *c.* 1794–5. Ministerio de la Gobernacias, Madrid. Photo Mas.

8 Witches on their broomsticks. A marginal illustration to Martin Lefranc, *Le Champion des Dames, c.* 1451. Cabinet des estampes, fonds français 12476, f. 150 v. Bibliothèque Nationale, Paris.

9 The Wicked Witch of the West. Film still from *The Wizard of Oz*, Metro-Goldwyn-Mayer, 1939. Photo Cinema Bookshop, London.

10 *Conjuro*. Oil painting by Francisco Goya, *c.* 1974–5. Lazaro Galdeano Museum, Madrid. Photo Mas.

11 Sybil Leek, a modern witch. Photo Associated Press, London.

17 Wooden puppet from the Congo. Museum of Mankind, London.

19 Sixteenth-century brown Bellarmine jug containing a cloth heart stuck with pins, some human hair and nail parings. Excavated in 1904 at Westminster. Pitt Rivers Museum, Oxford.

20 Sick Sia Indian boy undergoing treatment in ceremonial chamber. Photographed *c.* 1888–9 by Matilda Stevenson. Smithsonian Institution, Washington.

21 Witch-doctor of the Zande tribe. Photographed in the late 1920s by E. Evans-Pritchard. Pitt Rivers Museum, Oxford.

23 Witch-mask from the Sankuru River area. Museum of Mankind, London.

26 Voodoo dancers in Haiti. Photo Guido Mangold, Camera Press (Sven Simon), London.

Rapedi Letsebe, magician and rainmaker of the Kgatla tribe in Botswana, with his divining bones. Photographed in the 1920s by I. Schapera. Reproduced with permission of the Royal Anthropological Institute.

28 Three witches changing their shape and flying on a broomstick. From Ulrich Molitor, *Tractatus von den bösen Weibern*, 1495.

30 Painted terracotta plaque of the goddess Lilitu, early second millennium BC. Photo courtesy of Sotheby, Parke Bernet and Co., London.

32 Satyrs with Dionysus and a maenad on an amphora by the Amasis painter, sixth century BC. Antikenmuseum, Basel.

34 Quetzalcoatl, front and back views. Mexico, AD 900–1250. Courtesy of the Brooklyn Museum, New York, Henry L. Batterman and Frank Sherman Benson Funds.

36 Fall of the rebel angels. From St Augustine, *City of God*, French manuscript, fourteenth century. Bibliothèque Nationale, Paris.

38 *La Cocina de las Brujas*. Oil painting by Francisco Goya, *c.* 1794–5. Whereabouts unknown. Photo Mas.

39 Various aspects of the sabbat. Frontispiece to Collin de Plancy, *Dictionnaire Infernal*, 1863.

40 Antler-headed Celtic god. Detail from the Gundestrup cauldron. Danish, second or first century BC. Nationalmuseet, Copenhagen.

41 Anglo-Saxon bronze buckle excavated at Finglesham, Kent. Institute of Archaeology, Oxford.

43 Animal head from the corner post of Shetelig's sledge. From the ninth-century Oseberg ship burial

find. University Museum of National Antiquities, Oslo.

44 Anglo-Saxon magician, early eleventh century. MS Cotton Tiberius B.V. part 1, f. 87 v. British Library, London.

46 Witches making rain. Woodcut from Ulrich Molitor, *De Lamiis et Phitonicis Mulieribus*, 1490.

47 Diana (Artemis), Greek, fourth century B C. National Museum of Naples. Photo Mansell-Alinari.

48 Hecate. From Vincenzo Cartari, *Les Images des Dieux*, 1610.

49 A wild man, wild woman and their baby, outside their cave. Painting by Jean Bourdichon, fifteenth century. Ecole Nationale Supérieure des Beaux-Arts, Paris.

51 Palaeolithic cave drawing of a stag or dancer in stag costume, from the cave of the Trois Frères, Ariège, France. Drawing after Abbé Breuil.

Herne the Hunter. Engraving by George Cruikshank, 1843.

52 Illustration to an account of the witch trial at Warboys, Huntingdonshire. From Richard Boulton, *The History of Magic*, 1715–16.

56 Pact with the Devil. From Francesco Mario Guazzo, *Compendium Maleficarum*, 1608.

Theophilus pays homage to the devil who holds the written contract. From *The Psalter of Queen Ingeborg of Denmark*, before 1210. Musée Condé, Chantilly, MS 1695, f. 35 v. Photo Giraudon.

57 Title page from Christopher Marlowe, *Dr Faustus*, 1620.

59 Witches roasting and boiling children. From Francesco Mario Guazzo, *Compendium Maleficarum*, 1608.

61 *Auto-da-fé.* Painting by P. Berruguete, sixteenth century. Prado, Madrid. Photo Mas.

63 The obscene kiss. From Francesco Mario Guazzo, *Compendium Maleficarum*, 1608.

65 The witch of Berkeley being carried off by the Devil. From Hartmannus Schegel, *Registrum Hujus Operis Libri Chronicarum*, 1493.

66 Christ defending the City of God against Satan, twelfth century. MS Laud. Misc. 469, f. 7 v. Bodleian Library, Oxford.

67 *The Nightmare.* Painting by Henry Fuseli, 1781. Goethe Museum, Frankfurt-am-Main.

68 The Devil embracing a woman. From Ulrich Molitor, *De Lamiis et Phitonicis Mulieribus*, 1490.

69 Witches being hanged From Ralph Gardiner, *England's Grievance Discovered in Relation to the Coal Trade*, 1655.

71 Several methods of torture used before the Inquisitor. From M. Molinos, *The Persecution of the Famous Molinos, c.* 1745.

74 Waldensian heretics. Frontispiece to the French translation of Johannes Tinctoris, *Tractatus Contra Sectum Valdensium*, fifteenth century. Cabinet des manuscripts, fonds, français 961. Bibliothèque Nationale, Paris.

75 *Synagogue.* Outer panel of the *Heilsspiegel* altarpiece by Conrad Witz, *c.* 1435. Kunstmuseum, Basel.

77 The burning of Jacques de Molay and a companion in 1313. From *Chroniques de France*, end of fourteenth century. MS Royal 20 C. VII, f. 48. British Library, London.

80 Swimming a witch. Title page from *Witches apprehended, examined and executed, for notable villanies by them committed both by land and water*, 1613. Bodleian Library, Oxford.

81 Writing down a confession during torture. From, *Bamberger Halsgerichtordnung*, 1508. Historical Museum, Bamberg. Photo Emil Bauer.

85 Johann Wier or Weyer (1515–88). Anonymous engraving, sixteenth century. Bibliothèque Nationale, Paris.

86 The witch-house at Bamberg. Engraving 1627. Historical Museum, Bamberg. Photo Emil Bauer.

88 The execution of Urbain Grandier. Woodcut 1634. Bibliothèque Nationale, Paris.

91 A witch and her familiars. From *A Discovery of Witchcraft*, 1621. Add MS 32496, f. 2. British Library, London.

93 Anonymous portrait of John Dee, 1594. Ashmolean Museum, Oxford.

95 The execution of three Chelmsford witches, 1589. Reproduced by permission of His Grace the Archbishop of Canterbury and the Trustees of Lambeth Palace Library.

96 King James I of England, 1610. A painting probably by John de Critz. Reproduced by permission of the Trustees of the National Maritime Museum, Greenwich.

98 The Lancashire witches. From a tract, *The Famous History of the Lancashire Witches*, 1780.

99 Frontispiece to Matthew Hopkins, *The Discoverie of Witches*, 1647. By permission of the Master and Fellows, Magdalene College, Cambridge.

101 Frontispiece to the third edition of Joseph Glanvill, *Sadducismus Triumphatus*, 1689. First published in 1681.

102 *Black John chastising the Witches*. From George Cruikshank, *Twelve Sketches Illustrative of Sir Walter Scott's Demonology and Witchcraft*, 1830.

104 Cotton Mather (1662–1728). Engraving by W. J. Alais. Courtesy of the Essex Institute, Salem, Massachusetts.

107 Title page of Increase Mather, *A Further Account of the Tryals of the New England Witches . . .*, 1963.

110 Witches offer a child to the Devil. From Francesco Mario Guazzo, *Compendium Maleficarum*, 1608.

114 *The Sabbat*. Oil painting by Francesco Goya, *c.* 1794–5. Lazaro Galdeano Museum, Madrid. Photo Mas.

117 Title page to the 1669 edition of J. Sprenger and H. Institoris, *Malleus Maleficarum*.

119 Map of Salem Village in 1692. Drawn in 1866 by W. P. Upham, using original material. Courtesy of the Essex Institute, Salem, Massachusetts.

121 *The Trial of George Jacobs for Witchcraft*. Painting by T. H. Matteson. Courtesy of the Essex Institute, Salem, Massachusetts.

123 The witches of Mora, Sweden, being burnt. Engraving 1670. Kungliga Biblioteket, Stockholm.

125 René Descartes. Anonymous engraving.

127 Title page from Francis Hutchinson, *An Historical Essay Concerning Witchcraft . . .* , 1720.

129 *La Lampara del Diablo*. A scene from *El Hechizado por Fuerza*. Oil painting by Francisco Goya, *c.* 1794–5. National Gallery, London.

130 Man consulting a witch. Engraving from the Douce Collection. Bodleian Library, Oxford.

132 *Sir Francis Dashwood Worshipping Venus*. Engraving after a painting by Hogarth. British Museum, London.

134 The Sabbatic Goat. Engraving from Eliphas Lévi, *Transcendental Magic, its Doctrine and Ritual*, 1896.

135 *Self-portrait* by Aleister Crowley. Photo Radio Times Hulton Picture Library.

136 Leila Waddell, branded with the mark of the beast, *c.* 1912. Photo Radio Times Hulton Picture Library.

MacGregor Mathers, head of the Order of the Golden Dawn. Photo Radio Times Hulton Picture Library.

137 Pan teaching Olympus to play the pipes. Pompeii, first century AD. National Museum of Naples. Photo Mansell-Alinari.

139 Alex Sanders, leader of the Alexandrians. Photo John Hedgecoe/M. Magazine, Camera Press, London.

141 An invitation to a wedding. Courtesy of the author.

145 Portrait photograph of Anton Szandor La Vey. Photo courtesy of Anton Szandor La Vey.

147 Charles Manson. Photo Ray Hamilton, Camera Press, London.

149 Sybil Leek casting a 'good spell' over the countryside near her home in Hampshire. Photo Associated Press, London.

150 Title page of Charles Leland, *Aradia*, 1899.

151 Drawing of a witch. From Charles Leland, *Etruscan-Roman Remains in Popular Tradition*, 1892.

153 Dr Gerald Gardner with some of the items from his witchcraft collection, 1951. Photo courtesy of E. W. Kinrade.

155 Alex Sanders leading a ritual dance. Photo John Moss, Camera Press, London.

156 Bobbie, a California witch. Photo courtesy of George Patterson.

162 Black magic signs fixed on the church door at Castle Rising, Norfolk, 1963. Photo Lynn News and Advertiser.

167 *Witch Couple*. Drawing by Dirk Dykstra, 1978. Courtesy of the artist.

168 *Wiccaning*. Drawing by Dirk Dykstra, 1978. Courtesy of the artist.

169 A meeting of a California coven of witches. Photo courtesy of George Patterson.

170 George Patterson, a California witch. Photo courtesy of George Patterson.

Magic circle in the garden of George Patterson. Photo courtesy of George Patterson.

175 *Les Lupins* (detail). Lithograph by E. Vernier, after Maurice Sand, 1858. An illustration for George Sand, *Les Légendes Rustiques*, 1858. Bibliothèque Nationale, Paris.

Index

Page numbers in *italics* refer to illustrations

Ad Extirpanda, bull 70
Adler, Margot 171
Africa 8, 14, 18, 20–29, 72, 92, 97, *17, 23, 26*
age, correlation with witch accusations 22, 110, 113–14
Aix-en-Provence, case of Catherine Cordière at 131; nuns of 88
Alan of Lille 62
Alexander IV, pope 71
Alexandrians, *see* Sanders, Alex
America 103; modern witchcraft in 139–75; *see also* Salem
Anath 158
angels, fall of *36*
Anglo-Saxon sorcery 45, *44*
Apocalyptic Judaism 33–5
Aquinas, Thomas 70
Aradia, see Leland, Charles
Aristotelianism 73, 125
arson 103, 113
Association of Cymmry Wicca 155
Astarte 158
astrology 161, 173
athame 166, 169–71
Augustine of Hippo, Saint 39, 70, *36*

Babylonia 29
Bacchanalia 32, *32*
Bakweri, African tribe 25
Balingen 111
Bamberg, witch-house of 81, 86, 172, *87*
Basuto, African tribe 22
Bayley, James 120
Bechuana, African tribe 22
Benandanti 76
Benevento 53
Berkeley, witch of 64, *65*
Berta, goddess 49–50

Berwick 94–7
black mass 11, 128–31, 172
Blackwood, Algernon 133
Blocula, *see* Mora
Bodin, Jean 84
Bogomils 60
Boguet, Henri 84
bonae mulieres 53
Bonewits, Isaac *141*
Boniface VIII, pope 76
Book of Shadows 158, 166; Gardner's 154
Boyer, Paul, and Stephen Nissenbaum 15, 24, 106, 109, 118–21
Bronze Age 42
broomsticks, *see* flying
Bulwer-Lytton, Edward 133
burning, punishment 69–70, 83–4, 96, 172, *88*
Burroughs, George 106
Bury St Edmunds 102

Cabbala 148
Caesarius of Heisterbach 64
Calvin and Calvinism 82, 97
Calw 126
Campbell, Candice Haddad 157
Candlemas 50, 167
candles 166, 169
Canidia and Sagana 30
cannibalism 37, 55, 59, 78, *59*; worldwide motif 22
Canon Episcopi 53–4, 73, 76, 124
Caroline Code of law 82–3, 111
Cathars 60–62, 66, 78, 115, 152, *61*
cats, as familiars 90, 93–4, 100, 144, *91*; as form of Diana 152; at sabbats 37, 62; black cats as shape of witches 27–8, 64, 102; sexual intercourse with women 22
cauldron 166

Celtic religion 40, *40*
Cernunnos 156
Cerridwen 158
chalice 166, 169
Chambre ardente affair 128–31
Charlemagne 53
Chelmsford, Essex 92–4, 100, 112
children in witch accusations 83–4, 110, 118–22, *110*
Christianity, renunciation of 37, 55, 64, 78–9, 102
Church of Wicca 164
cingulum 166, *168*
Circe 30, 115
Clarke, Arthur C. 161
Clarke, Ursula 103
Clerk, Jane 122
Cohn, Norman 15
coincidence of opposites 158–9, 167
Colmar 82
cone of power 157, 170
confiscation 83
Connecticut 103
Cordière, Catherine 131
Cory, Martha 105
coven 102; in modern witchcraft 157, 163, 165–6, 169–71; origin of term 76
Covenant of the Goddess 155
Crotona, Fellowship of 153
Crowley, Aleister 133–6, 153–4, 161, *134, 136*
crucifix or sacraments, desecration of 37, 55, 78–9, 86–7, 130
cunning-folk, witch-finders 97
curanderos, witch-doctors 25
Cybele 32
Cyprian, modern witch 161
Cyrano de Bergerac 126

Daly, Mary 156
Dashwood, Sir Francis 131, *132*

death penalty 32, 53, 69–70, 122, 61; *see also* burning, hanging
Dee, John 92, *93*
Delcambre, Etienne 79–80
demography, correlation with witchcraft 112
demons 30
Descartes, René 124, *125*
Devil, Devil's mark 80–82, 86, 94, 102; meaning of word 33
Diana 46, *47*; as demon 39; as fertility goddess 48; as Hecate 48, 116, *48*, associated with the Wild Hunt 49, 53–4, 76; in modern witchcraft 151–2, 156
Dianus 41, 152, 160
Dionysos 31–2, *32*
divination 18, 97, 161, *26*
dogs 37, 90, 100, 142, *91*
Dominicans 72, 79, 83
Douglas, Mary 15
drawing down the moon 154, 163, 170
Druidism 159–61
dualism, *see* Cathars, Iran

Edda 45–6
Edward I, of England 76
Edward II, of England 76
Egbert, confessional of 45
Egypt 29
Eliade, Mircea 173
Elymas (Bar-Jesus) 35–6
England 76, 79, 82, 90–103, 122; modern witchcraft in 139–75; *see also* Anglo-Saxon sorcery
Enlightenment 124–6
Eostre 167
esbat 163, 168
Essex 92–4, 98–100, 111
ethics of modern witches 160
Evans-Pritchard, E. E. 14, 20, 21, *21*
Exodus, book of 53

familiars 52, 84, 90, 100, 105, *52*, *91*, *95*, *99*; modern 142, 144; sucking witches' teats 81; worldwide motif 22; *see also* cats, dogs
family, importance of in witchcraft accusations 24, 112, 118–21

Faust 55, *57*
female evil spirits 29–31, *30*
feminist witches 148–75
ferrets 94
festivals, *see* holidays
Flade, Dietrich 83–4
flying 37, 55, 64, 79, 84, 92, 102, *8*, *39*, *98*; standard charge 82; worldwide motif 22
folklore as element in witchcraft 46, 50, 52, 54, 63–5
Francis, Elizabeth 92–4
Franklin, Benjamin 131
Frazer, Sir James 41, 133, 148
Friuli 76

Gardner, Gerald 136, 152–5, 157, 161–2, 166, 169, *153*
Germany, modern witchcraft in 140–44
Gervaise of Tilbury 64
Gilles de Rais 78
Ginzburg, Carlo 76
Girard, Jean-Baptiste 131
Glanvill, Joseph 100, 102, *101*
gnosticism 33, 59–60, 62
goat 74, *115*
Goddess, the 53–4; in modern witchcraft 151–75
goeteia 30
Goethe, Johann 55
Goode, Sarah 105–6
Gowdie, Isobel 102–3, *102*
Goya, Francisco de 8, 126, *frontispiece, 2, 10, 38, 114, 129*
Graeco-Roman sorcery 29–32, 42
Grandier, Urbain 88–9, *88*
Graves, Robert 152–3
Greeley, Andrew 156
Gregory IX, pope 71
grimoires 131, 134, 142–4; Gerald Gardner's 153
Gui, Bernard 76
Guichard of Troyes 76

Hallowe'en 50, 168
hanging 69, 94, 104–8, 172, *69, 95*
Harpies 31
Harvestide festival 168
Hasler, Bernadette 142

Hausmannin, Walpurga 84
Hebrew religion 33–5, 42
Hebrew sorcery 32–3
Hecate, *see* Diana
Hellfire Club 131, *132*
Henry VI, of England 90
Henry VIII, of England 109; *see also* Statute of 1542
herbology 161
heresy, and Satanism 140; and sorcery 52; as formative element in witchcraft 24, 41, 55–63, 113, 172; function of 109; in England 76, 90; punishment for 53, 69, 70, 83; witchcraft defined as 73–8, 115, *74*; *see also* Cathars, Waldensians
Hermetic Order of the Golden Dawn 133–6, 140, 153
Herne 'the Hunter' 50, *51*
Herodias, identified with Wild Hunt 49
Hertfordshire 128
hexenbanner 97, 142–4
High Priest and Priestess in modern witchcraft 154, 163, 165–6, 170
Hilda (Holda, Hille, Hulda) 42, 49, 53–4, 76
Hincmar of Reims 55
Hindremstein, Dorothea 112
historical interpretations of witchcraft 15, 40–44, 124
holidays 50, 167–8
Hopkins, Matthew 97–100, *99*
Horned God 158–9, 161, 166, 169–70
horses 27
Hume, David 124
Hutchinson, Francis 100, 126, *127*
Huysmans, J. K. 133

illness, correlated with witchcraft 111
Imbolc, *see* Candlemas
incubi and succubi 29, 64, 82, *67*
infanticide 37, 55, 78, 130, *39, 59, 110*; at Orleans 58–9; worldwide motif 22
initiation, 37; in modern witchcraft 163–6
Innocent III, pope 70

Innocent IV, pope 70
Innocent VIII, pope 79, 82
inquisition 55, 69–72, 76–9, 113, 56, 71
Institoris, Heinrich 79, 116–18, 117
Iran, source of dualism 29, 33, 35, 152
Ireland 90–92
Ishtar 158
Isis 158

Jacobs, George 121
James, E. O. 152, 153
James I and VI, of England and Scotland 33, 79, 94, 96, 100, 102, 122, 96; see also King James Bible, Statute of 1604
January, festival of 50, 51
Jarcke, Karl-Ernst 131–3
Jews 75
Joan of Arc 78
John XXII, pope 76
Jung, Carl 158–9, 173
Junius, Johannes 86–7
Jura Mountains 83

Kali 158
Kelly, Aidan 153–4, 169
Kelly, Tony 157
Kieckhefer, Richard 15, 78
King James Bible 33, 96–7
Kruse, Johann 142–4
Kyteler, Alice 90–92

Labartu, evil spirit 29
lamias 31, 48
Lammas 168
Lamothe-Langon, Etienne de 133
Lancashire witches 97, 98
LaVey, Anton Szandor 144–6, 145
law, and standard lists of witch accusations 82; and status of sorcery in early Europe 52–4; and tests for witchcraft 80–81; Anglo-Saxon 53; canon law 52–4, 69; civil law 69; courts 77; Germanic 70; in British Isles 92–103; in church councils 52–4; in witch-craze 82–7; Roman

52, 69–70; Visigothic 46; see also Statutes
Leek, Sybil 148, 11, 149
Leland, Charles 148–53, 159, 169, 150, 151
Leptinnes, council of 52
Lévi, Eliphas 133, 134
Leviticus, book of 53
Lilith (Lilitu) 29, 31, 30
loa (Voodoo gods) 27
Lombards 53
Lombardy 77–8
Lords of the Towers 169
Lorraine, French province 79–80
Loudun 73, 88–9, 126, 88
Louis XIV 11, 89, 128–31
Louviers 73, 89, 126
Lucerne 112
Lucifer 144, 152, 159
Luciferans 73, 75
Lugbara, African tribe 18
Lughnasad, see Lammas
Luther 82, 116
lynching 128

Macbeth 79
Macfarlane, Alan 15, 109, 111
Machen, Arthur 133
macumba 20
magic, and science 13; high magic 13–14; low magic 14; term 'magic' 12, 29
magic circle 157, 169–70, 130
Magna Mater 32, 158
Maiden, office in modern witchcraft 170
Malebranche, Nicolas de 125–6
malefica, maleficia, maleficus 86, 92, 100, 105; as heresy 77; in England 76; meaning of term 14, 32, 52, 55, 128; penalty for 53
Malleus Maleficarum 68–9, 79, 82, 92, 116–18, 117
Manson, Charles 8, 146, 147
Map, Walter 62
Marlowe, Christopher 55, 57
Marxism 133
Mather, Cotton 103–6, 108, 104
Mather, Increase 106–8, 107
Mathers, MacGregor 133–4, 136
May Eve (Beltane; Walpurgis-nacht) 50, 167–8

Mazdaism, see Iran
Medea 30, 115
meetings 37, 39, 46, 50, 55, 58; modern 157–75; 'sabbats' 82, 84, 86; 'synagogues' 78; worldwide motif 22
mental illness, correlated with witchcraft 110–11
Meyer, Anton 41
mice 100
Michel, Anneliese 142
Michelet, Jules 133, 148, 151
Middle Ages and witchcraft 72, 82
Midelfort, Erik 15, 109, 111, 113, 119
Midsummer Eve 50, 168
Midwest Pagan Council 155
midwives 84, 112, 115
moles 100
Molland, Alice 122
Mone, Franz-Josef 133
Montaigne, Michel Eyquem de 73, 125
Monter, E. William 15, 83, 109, 119
Montespan, Madame de 130
moon, in modern witchcraft 161, 168; see also Diana
Mora, in Sweden 122, 126, 123
'Moses', 'Sixth and Seventh Books of' 142–4
mountain origins of witchcraft 72
Murray, Margaret 41–2, 133, 152, 154, 156–7, 159–60, 168

natural disasters, correlated with witchcraft 111
nature, in modern witchcraft 157–75
ndakó-gboyá dancers 25
neighbours, and witchcraft 112
Neoplatonism 73
New Testament 35–6
New Wiccan Church 164
Norse religion 42–6, 43
nudity, in modern witchcraft 168–70, 155, 169
Nupe, African tribe 25
Nyakyusa, African tribe 25
Nyoro, African tribe 25

obscene kiss 37, 62, 94, *63*, *74*
Oenothea 30
ointments (salves) 37, 84, 90, 102, *39*, *59*; in *Malleus* 79; standard charge 82; worldwide motif 22
Order of the Temple of the Orient (O.T.O.) 133
orgy 37, 55, 78, 92, 144; in *Malleus* 79; modern 172; at Orleans 58–9; worldwide motif 22
Orleans, trial at (1022) 58–9, 62, 65
Osborne, Sarah 105

pact, as central doctrine of witchcraft 55, 66, 77–8; explicit 11, 55, 84, *56*; implicit 70, 73, 76–7; in England 92, 97, 102; origin of 55–9; witch of Berkeley and 64; *see also* Theophilus
Pagan Front 155
paganism, equated with demonolatry 52–3; meaning of term 40, 159
Pagan Movement 155
Pan 136, 159, *137*
pantheism 158
Paris, synod of 53
Paris, University of 77
Parris, Samuel 103–8; 120–21
Patterson, George *170*
Paul the Deacon 55
penitentials 45
pentacle paten 169
pentagram 169
Persephone 158
Philip IV, of France 76–7
pigs 27
Pondo, African tribe 25
Poor Law, in England 128
Prentice, Joan (Jane) 94, *95*
pricking, as test of witchcraft 80–81, 92
Protestantism 82–3, 116, 122, 124
Providence, Rhode Island 103
psychology of witchcraft 73
Putnam family 120–21

Quetzalcoatl 33, *34*

Reformation, as period of witchcraft 72
reincarnation, in modern witchcraft 161
Renaissance, as period of witchcraft 72–3
reputations, correlated with witchcraft 111–12
Robbins, Rossell Hope 83, 100
Rome, synod of (743) 53; synod of (826) 53
Rose, Elliot 41, 100, 148
Rosicrucians 133
Rudolf II, of Austria 83

sabbat, 62, *28*; modern 140, 163, 167–9
sacraments, desecration of, *see* crucifix
Sadducismus triumphatus, see Glanvill, Joseph
saints 40, 52–3
Salem 15, 24, 103–8, 110, 126, 172, *104*, *107*, *119*, *121*; social history of 118–21
salt, in modern witchcraft 169
Samhain, *see* Hallowe'en
Sampson, Agnes 94–6
Sanders, Alex 154, *139*, *155*
Satanism 8, 58, 140, 144–7, 163, 165, 172
Schismatic Druids of North America 160
Scot, Reginald 96
Scotland 76, 82, 92–103, 122
Scott, Walter 133
Sebald, Hans 142–4
secrecy 37, 165
sex, in modern witchcraft 170; *see also* incubi, orgy
shape-shifting 59, 64, 102, 105, *28*; in *Malleus* 79; Palaeolithic *51*; Voodoo 27–8; worldwide motif 22
'skyclad', *see* nudity
Smythe, Ellen 94
social class, correlated with witchcraft 111
social function of origins of the witch-craze 72; of sorcery 14–15, 19–22, 24–5, 42; of European

witchcraft 109–21; of Salem witchcraft 118–21; of witchcraft in the modern world 172–5
Somerset 102
sorcery 14–15, 18–26, 55, 128; and hanging 69; conflated with heresy 52–3, 70; in early Europe 42–52; persistence of past Middle Ages 123, 131, 140–44; term 'sorcery' 12, 14, 172; translated into witchcraft 63–6, 78
spells and charms 42, 45
Sprenger, Jakob 79
squirrels 100
Stanton, Margery 112
Stoker, Bram 133
Statutes, English *162*; of 1542 92, 122; of 1563 92, 97, 122; of 1604 97, 100, 122; of 1736 103, 122, 128; of 1951 (Fraudulent Mediums Act) 122
strappado 81, 86, *71*, *81*
striga, stria 53
Sufism 148
Summers, Montague 108
Summis Desiderantes Affectibus, bull 79, 82
Summoner, office in modern witchcraft 170
Super Illius Specula, bull 76
'supernatural', meaning of 12–13
'superstition', meaning of 12
swimming, test for witchcraft 80, *80*
sword, in modern witchcraft 169
'synagogue' 62, 78, *75*

Templars 76–7, *77*
Teufelsdreck (asafoetida) 143
Teutonic religion 40–50, 53, *41*, *43*
Theodore, penitential of 45
Theodosius, code of 69
theology, scholastic 66–73, *66*
Theophilus 55, *56*
theurgy 29
Thirty Years War 84–5, 128
Thomas, Keith 15
thurible 169
Tinctoris, Johannes *74*
Tituba 105, 108
Todi 112

torture 71, 81, 87; authorized by Innocent IV 70; function of 112; in English law 106; legal practice of 73, 77–82, 84, 86–7; see also strappado
Trevor-Roper, Hugh 121
Trier 83–4

ugliness, correlated with witchcraft 109–10

Vallin, Pierre 78–9
Voodoo 8, 20, 27–9, 26

Waite, A. E. 133
Waldensians 71, 75, 78, 115, 74
Walpurgisnight, see May Eve
Walter, bishop of Lichfield and Coventry 76
wand, in modern witchcraft 169

Warboys, witches of 52
'warlock' 12
Waterhouse, Agnes 92–4
weather-witching 84, 144, 46
Webster, John 100
weighing, as test of witchcraft 80
Wenham, Jane 10?, 122
Weston, Jessie 133
Weyer (Wier), Johann 84, 97, 85
White Goddess, see Graves, Robert
wicca, see witch
wiccaning 168
Wild Hunt 48–50, 46, 49, 51
wild men and women 46, 49
Willard, John 106
William of Malmesbury 64
William of Newburgh 63
witch, meaning of word 8, 12, 14, 33, 172, 177
Witchcraft Research Association 155

witch-doctors 8, 24–5
witch's mark 81, 92, 105
wizard, meaning of word 12
wolves 27–8, 64
women in witchcraft, archetype 116–18; followers of Diana 53–4; in Africa 22, 24; in Malleus 68–9, 79, 115–16; prevalence of 37, 84, 113–18; stereotype 11, 68; worldwide motif 22; see also feminist witches
Women's International Terrorist Conspiracy from Hell 155–6
worldwide traits of witchcraft 22–4

Yeats, William Butler 133
Yule 167

Zande, African tribe 20–22, 21